Early praise for *The Nature of*

This book should be "The CTO's Guide to ~~~~
ment." This is a book every CTO, every VF
of software, and every software team leade   ~~~. in this book
they'll find answers to questions that have plagued their peers for decades.
The book is simple and direct, and yet it tackles one of the most complicated tasks that humans have ever attempted: managing teams that build
high-quality software systems.

➤ **Robert "Uncle Bob" Martin, founder, Object Mentor**

Ditch the buzzword-laden books and read this instead. Ron takes us back
to development basics with a great summary of a simple development
process that works. Ron shows you just what's important in software development. If you're doing more than this, you're trying too hard.

➤ **Jeff Langr, author,** *Pragmatic Unit Testing in Java 8 with JUnit* **and**
 Modern C++ Programming With Test-Driven Development

The Nature of Software Development is just like spending a morning with
Ron, only you don't have to.

➤ **Chet Hendrickson**
 Agile Teacher and Consultant, HendricksonXP

I love this book. Every page has a sketch and a clear explanation of
something you can try out right away. It's like sitting down with Ron over
a cup of coffee.

➤ **Daniel H Steinberg**
 Dim Sum Thinking

In straightforward prose and sketches, Ron explores the deep question of
how to best deliver software. This book is accessible not just to software
team members, but to customers and users as well.

➤ **Bill Wake**
 Industrial Logic, Inc.

The Nature of
Software Development

Keep It Simple,
Make It Valuable,
Build It Piece by Piece

Ron Jeffries

The Pragmatic Bookshelf

Dallas, Texas • Raleigh, North Carolina

Many of the designations used by manufacturers and sellers to distinguish their products are claimed as trademarks. Where those designations appear in this book, and The Pragmatic Programmers, LLC was aware of a trademark claim, the designations have been printed in initial capital letters or in all capitals. The Pragmatic Starter Kit, The Pragmatic Programmer, Pragmatic Programming, Pragmatic Bookshelf, PragProg and the linking *g* device are trademarks of The Pragmatic Programmers, LLC.

Every precaution was taken in the preparation of this book. However, the publisher assumes no responsibility for errors or omissions, or for damages that may result from the use of information (including program listings) contained herein.

Our Pragmatic courses, workshops, and other products can help you and your team create better software and have more fun. For more information, as well as the latest Pragmatic titles, please visit us at *https://pragprog.com*.

The team that produced this book includes:

Michael Swaine (editor)
Potomac Indexing (indexer)
Liz Welch (copyeditor)
Dave Thomas (typesetter)
Janet Furlow (producer)
Ellie Callahan (support)

For international rights, please contact *rights@pragprog.com*.

Printed in the United States of America.
ISBN-13: 978-1-941222-37-9
Printed on acid-free paper.
Book version: P1.0—February, 2015

Contents

Preface viii

Acknowledgments x

Introduction xii

Part I — The Circle of Value

1. The Search for Value 4
2. Value Is What We Want 6
3. Guiding Goes Better "Feature by Feature" . . . 18
4. Organizing by Feature 26
5. Planning Feature by Feature 32
6. Building the Product, Feature by Feature . . . 42
7. Build Features and Foundation in Parallel . . . 50
8. Bug-Free and Well Designed 60
9. Full Circle 76

Part II — Notes and Essays

10. Value—What Is It? 80
11. Value—How Can We Measure It? 84
12. Of Course It's Hard! 88
13. Not That Simple 92
14. Creating Teams That Thrive 94
15. The "Five-Card Method" for Initial Forecasting . . 98
16. Managing Natural Software Development . . . 100
17. Whip the Ponies Harder 112
18. To Speed Up, Build with Skill 116
19. Refactoring 120
20. Agile Methods 126
21. Scaling Agile 130
22. Conclusion 148

Bibliography 150

Index 152

Preface

I've been doing software for over a half century. I've had some great successes and some truly colossal failures.

For all that time, I've been talking with people, coaching, and teaching about software development. And mostly, I've been thinking. I've been trying to figure out how this can all seem so simple and yet be so complex. If you've been involved in software development, you too have probably often felt that all this should be simple, but somehow it gets all complicated.

Thanks to being in the right place at the right time, I've been part of the Agile movement since the very beginning. That has drawn me back toward simplicity.

Like many of the best ideas in software development, modern "Agile" software development offers to make software development more productive and better controlled by making it simpler. Agile is simple. Four values, a dozen principles. How complex could it be? Well, it still seems to get pretty darn complex.

Agile methods like Scrum and XP are also simple. Again a few values, a couple of meetings, a handful of artifacts, how complex could they be? And still it gets so complicated so quickly.

What's up with that?

I have begun to see a way of looking at the whole process of software development. I'm starting to see a general overview that might help us keep things simple. Inside, there will still be plenty of complexity, but I hope this high-level map will help us pull back and find the simplicity when we find ourselves in the weeds.

Software development has many facets: determining value, managing value flow, organizing around the work, planning, building, and so on. Each of these facets needs to focus on producing value. Value needs to be visible so that it can be guided and managed. For this, we need to step back from the details and find the essential simplicity in this very complex activity.

When I think about things, I draw pictures that focus on some aspect of the topic. I try to think of a few words that will quickly focus my thinking when next I think about the topic. I use pictures to give me a different perspective. Since my drawings are perforce simple—I'm not very skilled—I use them to cut away complexity and look at what's left. I'm giving you a look at that thinking.

This book is an attempt at finding some essential simplicity inside the complex activity of building software products. I believe I have a handle on some good ideas. At best, this is a bit of a clearing along a tangled trail. Please take these thoughts and use them to find your own sense of simplicity amid all the chaos. Good luck!

Acknowledgments

...where to begin...where to end...

My parents, for freedom, trust, and a great library...

Sister Mary Marjorie, for a first taste of science; Mr. Dansky, for a first taste of love for a subject; the Jesuits, for showing the value of thinking and of course for my fashion sense.

Rick Camp, for inviting the kid up the street to be an intern at Strategic Air Command; Bill Rogers, for tossing me into programming and then helping me learn to swim.

Colleagues over the years: Charles Bair, Karen Dueweke, Steve Weiss, Gene Somdahl, Rick Evarts, Mike McConnell, Jean Musinski, Jeanne Hernandez, Dorothy Lieffers, Don Devine...it would take pages to mention everyone who has touched me.

Partners, mentors, colleagues in Agile: Ward Cunningham, Kent Beck, Chet Hendrickson, Ann Anderson, Bob Martin, Alistair Cockburn, Martin Fowler, Michael Feathers, Bob Koss, Brian Button, Brian Marick, Ken Schwaber, Jeff Sutherland, Ken Auer...I can't begin to list all those to whom I'm grateful.

The Internet and Twittersphere, who are surely tired of seeing me try to explain these thoughts so often.

Helpers with this book: Bill Tozier, Laura Fisher, and of course Chet Hendrickson, who has listened to and shaped every word. Any remaining errors are of course his fault.

The wonderful folks at The Pragmatic Programmers: Andy Hunt and Dave Thomas; Susannah Pfalzer, who knew when to manage me and when to stand back; Janet Furlow, who pushed the book through production; my patient and long-suffering editor, Mike Swaine—without these people there'd be no book.

My "boys," Ron and Mike, of whom I am most proud and who have filled my life with joy and events of interest.

And more than all of these, Ricia, my wife: without her nothing would seem worth doing. Thank you for taking care of me.

Thanks!

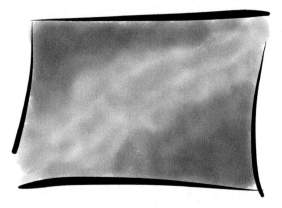

Software is Lava

Introduction

Kids often play a game: *The floor is lava*. In this game, you have to get from one place to another without touching the floor. Because the floor is lava. If you step in lava, you die, horribly, screaming. Don't step in lava. So, in the game, you must jump from the couch to the chair, crawl across the table, and leap to safety in the kitchen, where the floor is not lava.

Software is lava. Often it seems that there's no safe place to step. Worse yet, we're not allowed to jump on the furniture. Mom said. Sorry.

So what are we to do? As we build software, it seems that we're stepping in lava every day. It's complicated, it gets more complicated, and often it seems that we're just doomed.

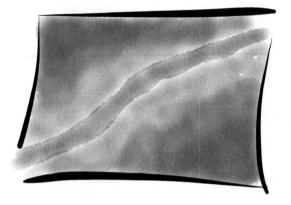

There has to be a better way.

We all feel it. We're all sure that there must be a way to build software that isn't lava. We didn't get there last time, but next time...*next time*...we'll get it right.

And, sure enough, next time, more lava. Ow! Die screaming.

Yet most of us have had moments when our feet weren't burning. There seem to be cool, grassy patches amid the lava. Sometimes we find them. It feels so good to be there.

The premise of this book is that there aren't just patches of grass—there is a cool, green, grassy path. Maybe we can't be on that path every moment, but understanding the path better is the way to a happier project.

I call that path "the Natural Way," because I believe that the path is built into a simple notion, a focus on delivering value early and often.

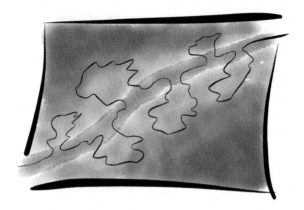

We will wander off the path.

Even though we much prefer to be on the grass than in the lava, it seems that we always get in the lava. (Sometimes lava is spelled differently. Anyway, we're in it.)

If there is a path—and I hope to show you that there is—we will wander off of it. Yes, we will. So as I describe the path to you, don't imagine that I believe we'll all be on the path and live happily ever after with no problems, with our grateful feet caressing the happy grasses of the path. We couldn't be that good, or that lucky.

What we can do is remain aware that there is a path. When we're not on the path, we'll think about value. We'll think about the Natural Way. And quite likely we'll be able to find our way back, if not to the grass, at least to a place where the lava isn't quite so hot.

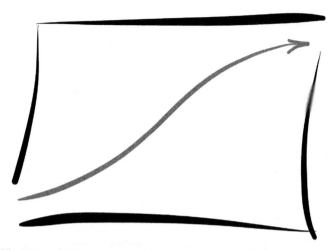

The Natural Way

The story in this book is a simple one: there is a *Natural Way* to build software, and it serves everyone well.

The Natural Way serves end users well because it delivers value to them sooner.

The Natural Way serves the business well because it provides a return on investment sooner, because it provides important information quickly, and because it provides the ability to adjust direction as needed.

The Natural Way serves management well too. It lets management see what's really going on inside the project so that when action is needed, there will be time to act. And it reduces management's problems by making information visible so that we don't have to dig for it.

The Natural Way even makes the job easier for developers. It provides them with clear direction and allows them freedom to use their skills to build what the organization needs, when it's needed.

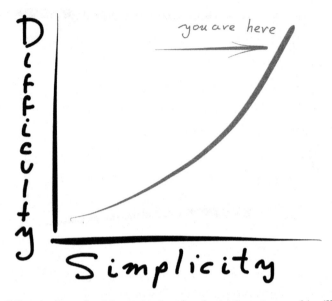

What is described here is simple—but it's not easy. You'll need to think about these ideas, to figure out how they'll be valuable to you, and to learn to do the things we explore here. Keep moving toward simplicity. You'll be glad you did.

The Natural Way does require us to think, to learn, and to change a bit. I think you'll see here that moving toward the Natural Way need not be traumatic. It can actually be quite a bit of fun.

Come along with me, and explore how we can make software development simpler by focusing on frequent delivery of visible value. We'll not talk about how things are, but how they might be, if we try.

A final warning before you jump in:

Channeling comedian Eddie Izzard's NSFW "Death Star Canteen" bit:

> This is not a book of what the heck to do!

It's not a book of recipes. It's not about one way to do something. That's not our purpose here. We're here to think about how things work, to ready ourselves for whatever may happen. There are many ways to accomplish what you need. I trust you to find ways, think of ways, and select among them.

Part I

The Circle of Value

Sometimes you just have to stop holding on with both hands, both feet, and your tail, to get someplace better. Of course you might plummet to the earth and die, but probably not: you were made for this.

VALUE

Successful software development is hard. It will always be hard. However, doing it smoothly and gracefully has a very real simplicity. Let's talk about that essential simplicity. As we do, your job is to think a lot, while I write very little.

CHAPTER 1

The Search for Value

This picture shows the flow of our argument here. Our story begins with value, and value is the point of our work:

Value. Value, we'll see, is "what you want." It can be any kind of value, from money to laughs or lives. We'll explore a bit about what value is.

We'll tell the story by building up from the bottom of the pyramid, describing how to guide, organize, plan, and build our product, in small slices, with a focus on quality. The value we produce is based on these.

Guiding. We produce value by creating teams with responsibility for creating value. We make sure they understand what is needed, and understand the time available. We guide them by observing what they actually build.

Organizing. We organize teams with the ability to get the job done. We organize around features, because features give us the ability to plan and build value most rapidly. We apply good people and help them build their skills.

Planning. We steer our projects by selecting the features we need, in the order we need them. We produce value in a timely fashion.

Building. We build up our product feature by feature. This provides frequent delivery of value. We can see how things are progressing early and often.

Slicing. We slice features down to the smallest possible value-bearing size. We build a capable product as early as possible, and then enhance and grow it as the deadline approaches. We're always ready to ship.

Quality. We apply the necessary practices to ensure that our product always has a good design and that it is as nearly defect-free as possible. We're able to build value continuously, sustainably, indefinitely.

What is software value?

CHAPTER 2

Value Is What We Want

We all want value. Value is what we want. Value is—*what we want*. In software, we generally get value by delivering features. Features that have value. Features that we want.

Often it's about money, because software can save time or money. Software can help us earn money. There are other kinds of value: software can make lives more convenient. Software can even save lives.

In the end, I think of value as simply *what we want*. We might like to put a number on value, but it's not necessary. As we build the software, we'll make choices. Each choice gives us something we value. We'll choose information, happy users, or saved lives. We'll choose what makes sense. We'll choose *what we want*.

Working incrementally, we'll choose the next thing we want. We'll have our team put it into the software, as quickly and solidly as they can. When they're done, we'll look to be sure we got what we want: we'll check for the value.

We'll say, "show us the software," to see the value.

What kinds of value does your project deliver to its users? To your organization? To the team? What value does it deliver to you?

NOW   LATER

Value starts when we ship the software.

A project delivers value only when we ship the software and put it to use. If we wait until we finish everything, it will be a long time before we get any value. Let's find a way to deliver value early.

We'd rather have the pony now, not later, but we can't create everything right now. We have many features in mind, and they'll take time to build. The more we want, the longer it takes.

What benefits could there be if we could deliver sooner? How might the organization benefit? What about the team? What about you and me?

What if we shipped some valuable part sooner than the rest?

Every product is made up of pieces. Call them features, or minimum marketable features. Call them aspects, functions, or capabilities. Each big piece has smaller pieces. Each is full of details that make that piece more complete, more useful, or just nicer.

Remember, most users of a product don't use every feature. There's some kind of 80/20 rule going on. Everyone may want something different, but no one wants everything. Even in the products you know best and use most, you probably use only a fraction of the features.

NOW

LATER?

Does shipping something small make sense?

Since most users don't use all the features, a smaller set of features can provide real value, and provide it sooner. Sometimes we think we have to have it all. Let's face it, though: if you've done very many software projects, you probably didn't get everything you wanted by the date you wanted it. We never get it all.

We can stamp our feet and demand a pony, or we can act like managers and steer our software projects to the best possible result. Very likely, there's a subset of capability that can start providing value sooner than the whole package. Let's find those features and ship them first. That way, we'll prosper.

After that first release, we may need to follow up with the rest of the product; otherwise, the final product may be worth less over its lifetime. So we'll usually plan multiple releases.

But there are times when we might just ship the first bit and then stop. When could that be the best thing to do? How many different reasons can you think of?

Deliver just one part and then stop?

If we ship just once, we'll get an earlier return, but it will probably be less than if we shipped the whole product, even later on. Or will it?

Information has value as well. Sometimes the most important information we can get is that we're doing the wrong thing. One very good way to find out if we're going in the right direction is to ship a small version of the product early. If it flops, we can change direction at low cost.

Usually, though, we do have a good idea. With a good idea, what kind of pieces should we work on? How would our product best be delivered a bit at a time? What should the pieces look like?

We must see and understand the pieces.

It's not enough for our teams to work on mysterious technical bits that make sense only to them.

We need to guide our teams to build pieces that make sense to us, and to our users. These are often called *minimal marketable features (MMFs)*. In fact, we'll often benefit from providing business direction at an even finer grain than the usual MMF.

Here, we'll call those pieces *features*. When we say "show us the software," we want to see features that we want and understand.

Looking back at some previous projects, what are some features you wish you could have shipped sooner, and why? What are some features that should have been different? Are there some that shouldn't have been done at all?

Value, by feature

Each feature that we might build adds some value to the product. And each one takes some amount of time. We can't know exactly how valuable or exactly how much time. But we can still get an excellent sense of what to do.

Suppose the height of the features is their value, and the width is their cost. Which ones should we build first, and which ones should we defer until later? Pretty clear, isn't it?

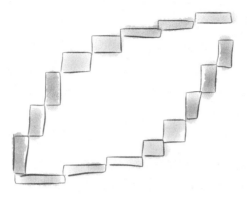

Value growth depends on what we choose to do.

Look at the difference in the growth of value if we choose the higher-value, inexpensive features first and defer lower-value, costly features until later. And these features only vary by about a factor of three to one. In most products the best ideas are tens of times better than the worst—or more. The results would hardly fit on the page!

Some of those later features look pretty boring. What would happen if we did different, more valuable features, even for some other product?

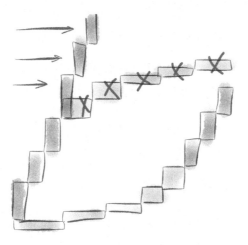

We might even switch our investment to a new product!

When we begin to ship frequently, with highest value first, the time soon comes when the next features aren't worth the time and money to create them. This is a good thing. We can often do far better by investing in a new product.

What's the next product we'd like to do? Who might feel negatively impacted by a product shift? How might we make that shift a good thing for everyone? Can we focus on a portfolio rather than separate products with diminishing returns? Can we show more software, with more value?

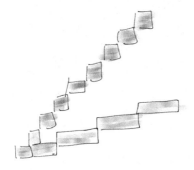

Best value comes from small, value-focused features, delivered frequently.

OK, we can see that small features could deliver value sooner if we can do them. Let's think next about managing our project. Will smaller visible results help us manage? How might they get in the way?

What about our teams? Are they organized to work this way? Do they have the people they need, the skills they need, and the help they need? Read on—we'll talk about all those things.

The main thing to remember is that we get the best results from delivering the software, feature by feature.

Further reading:

- Chapter 10, *Value—What Is It?*, on page 80
- Chapter 11, *Value—How Can We Measure It?*, on page 84

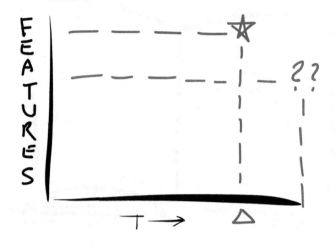

CHAPTER 3

Guiding Goes Better
"Feature by Feature"

The first thing we know about any project is the deadline — at least it always seems that way. That's the vertical blue line with the triangle at the bottom.

And what do we want by the deadline? Why, everything, of course. That's the horizontal line. The star is our plan: have everything by the deadline. No problem!

Somehow it doesn't turn out that way. We usually wind up shipping less, or later, or both: the red lines with the question marks. Heck, we're sure to get less than we want. After all, we asked for *everything!*

We really can't have it all. Let's manage that reality, not just let things happen. Let's steer our project, not just ride it wherever it takes us.

In a recent project of yours, what important things didn't get done? What got done that turned out to be wasted? What did you find out about too late, or nearly so?

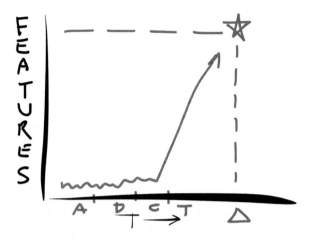

Conventional software projects proceed in phases.

Many projects plan with *activity-based* phases: Analysis, Design, Coding, and finally Testing. The green line is our plan for such a project, and it may look good. But even if we get Analysis done on time, that doesn't tell us how well we'll do on Design or Coding.

Until we begin to see the software, we can't really tell how well we're doing. And when we start getting and testing that code, what happens? Generally nothing good!

Have any of your projects given you too little time to react when trouble arose? Would there be value to knowing sooner what's really going on? Did you ever wish you could get at least some value out of all that effort?

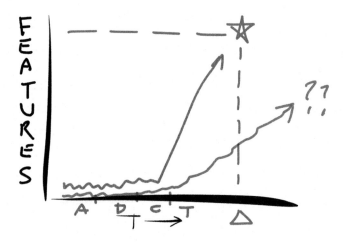

Worse yet, things rarely go according to plan.

Finally, we begin to see and test the code. And the facts aren't good. Inevitably we're later than we thought. We have less done than we thought. What we have done doesn't work very well.

We knew we had asked for more than we could do: that's the nature of goal setting. But by the time we find out where we are, it's too late to do much about it.

With more warning, maybe we could have shipped a subset on time. Now we have few choices. We could write the project off, but that would be career suicide. Or we can trudge gamely on, hoping to ship something before they give up on us.

Either way, we look bad. Either way, it *is* bad!

Have you ever had to ship in bad condition? Were there too many defects still in the software? Was the software too hard to change? Were important features missing? Important new ideas that it was too late to add?

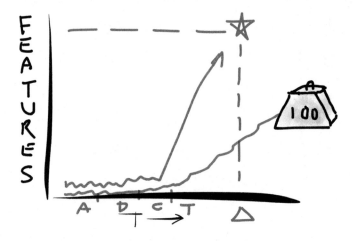

The activity-based product is a monolith.

With a monolithic project, late in the game we can't do much to cut costs. We have already written requirements for things we'll never get. We've designed and even written code for things that we'll never complete. All that work is wasted.

If only we had known the truth. We could have deferred some of that work.

We laid out this project with an all-or-nothing mentality. We analyzed it all. We designed it all. We tried to code it all. We discovered, too late, that we can't have it all.

Trying to plan and build it all has hurt us. We have no time to change, and even if we had time, we'd never untangle all the things we shouldn't have done from the things we should have.

Instead, let's plan for multiple releases from the very beginning. Multiple releases are easier to manage and deliver value sooner. It's even easier to build the software that way. Everyone wins.

Do those plan, analyze, design-code-test phases really help you manage your project? Wouldn't it be easier to manage things if you could just get the features, a few at a time, in the order you wanted them, starting right at the beginning? Let's look at that.

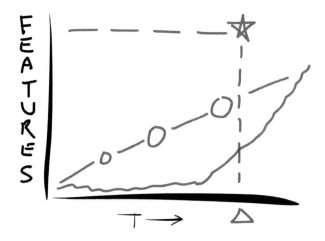

A project that delivers feature by feature is more predictable.

We've seen that delivering release by release, feature by feature, lets us ship value sooner. What about our ability to manage and guide the effort?

Our old red conventional project drones on and on, delivering too little information, too late. But the green project shows us real, valuable features at frequent intervals. We can see what is happening. We can see the software!

Can you see how a flow of visible features would be easier to manage? Can you see how you could maximize project value as you go?

What about risk? Can you see how to evaluate or reduce a project risk by building something visible? Can you see how to deal with a marketing risk with a small test feature?

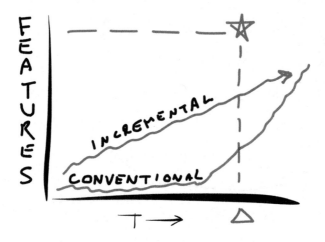

Feature by feature gives better information, better guidance, better results.

When we build our software projects feature by feature, things go better. We can see how much is done and how rapidly the project is progressing. We get a good sense of how much will be done by any given date.

We choose the most important features to do next. We build the best possible combination of features for any desired shipment date—even one earlier than our original desired date. We can even change features, adding new ones in response to better ideas or changing user needs.

When our projects grow feature by feature, we can respond to what's really happening. We can respond to the changing needs and inputs of the business and of management.

What would it take to make this way of working possible? How can we plan a project when we don't even know what we'll wind up wanting to do?

Further reading:

- Chapter 14, *Creating Teams That Thrive*, on page 94
- Chapter 16, *Managing Natural Software Development*, on page 100

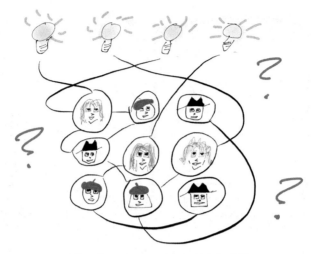

Building features requires multiple skills.

CHAPTER 4

Organizing by Feature

We want to get value in small bites: features. We prosper when we manage in terms of value, in terms of features.

How can we organize our work, and ourselves, for the best and most rapid flow of value?

To get the work done, different parts require different skills. The work won't be done—or at least not done well—until it has had the attention of people with each needed skill.

If we organize teams by skill-set, each piece of work will need to be passed around among teams. Each handoff will require scheduling and cause delays. Quite likely, problems will arise from each handoff.

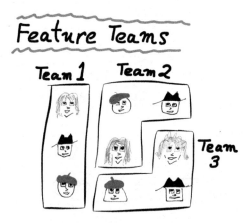

Teams build features.

The answer is simple: organize into small teams, each of which builds features that the Product Champions can understand. Make sure that each team has all the people and all the skills necessary to build the entire feature, not just part of it.

The advantages of this should be clear: we can allocate work across teams easily. We can see where everything is. Each feature gets dedicated attention. Responsibility and authority are aligned.

It's simple and works well. But it's not that easy, is it?

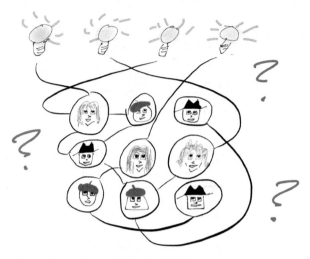

But...but...but we're not organized that way.

I know. And I'm here to say that you probably should be.

If each feature that you want must be passed through multiple teams, it takes longer and results in lower quality. Why? Because the teams need to be coordinated somehow, and each item has to be passed from one team to the next. After it's passed, it needs to sit in the queue for the next team to wait its turn. And often—very often—the feature needs to go back to the first team to fix something they didn't understand. Often it will go back and forth several times.

This slows you down.

Yes, feature teams may be a change for you. But if you want to go rapidly and smoothly, you'll very likely benefit from moving in that direction. Take your time, don't panic, but give it a try. Create a Feature Team, a darn good one. See whether fewer handoffs speed delivery and improve quality. I'm betting things will go better. If so, rinse, repeat.

We don't have enough specialists.

Maybe you don't have enough database experts or user experience (UX) experts. You couldn't possibly have one on every feature team. You might wind up with more things to do than teams to do them. It seems you can't create that next feature team that you need.

Well, maybe. I'll bet you have people who understand databases rather well even though you wouldn't call them "experts." You might even have some people who are experts and don't have the badge. You probably have plenty of people who can build an interface and get close to what your best UX people can do. They might even do better.

So here's a thought experiment: what if you create teams to build features, in order of most important features first? Since the team you're working on now has the most important features to do that aren't already being done, they clearly deserve the best database person and UX person you have next. Put them in there. Rinse, repeat.

Soon, you might find yourself creating a team whose database person, or UX person, really isn't quite good enough. Super. You've identified a training opportunity. A learning opportunity. An opportunity to form a guild, a Community of Practice!

Create Communities of Practice.

Now create a Database Community of Practice, or UX Community of Practice. Build it around the people who used to be in the database or UX group, and include all the people who are now charged with doing those things on your feature teams. This isn't a new department: the people belong to the feature teams.

They are also members of the Database or UX Community of Practice. You belong to your family; you're a member of the golf club.

Your senior people—not always the ones you thought were the senior people—now have an additional responsibility: bringing the less experienced people up to full speed. A highly paid expert shouldn't be highly paid just because she's an expert. She should be highly paid because she is helping other people become experts.

Your top people shepherd the less experienced ones. They drop into other teams and help them, making sure that the real team member retains responsibility and learns what needs to be done and how to do it. Soon you'll have all the experts you need—and happier people as well!

Feature teams make "scaling" easy.

We have a chapter on "scaling" coming up in Part II. The short message is this: much of your work can be done by a single cross-functional team. Most of the rest can be done by a number of feature teams working in parallel on features that you understand and desire.

There may be very little in your organization that really requires multiple teams working in lockstep. If you'll break out your work feature by feature, you'll quite likely discover that what's left is simple. This will save you from spending a fortune "scaling" into a structure and organization that will not serve you.

Organize by feature. You'll be glad you did.

Moving from vision to details

CHAPTER 5

Planning Feature by Feature

Things go best with frequent releases of software. Value grows faster and better. Management gets visible progress at short intervals. Development works best with small, clear objectives.

The product "vision," however, starts with big, grand ideas, vague yet enticing. Vision is about big ideas, not tiny bites.

How can we move from our grand product ideas down to those detailed features we need for the best visibility and control?

Planning is indispensable.

General Eisenhower said, "Plans are useless, but planning is indispensable." We do really need to think deeply about our product, not just at the beginning but all the time.

We do need to plan. We don't need a detailed list of what will happen and when. When the time comes, let's decide then what to do next. A too-detailed plan will just waste time and create confusion.

It's important to identify key features that we'll need to have early, as well as features we can't live without. Let's identify and record those.

We need to defer implementing low-value ideas indefinitely. Let's not waste time thinking about and keeping track of them.

Still, planning is important. We probably have to consider a lot of bad ideas to get a few good ones. So let's do plan but at the same time stay loose and ready for change.

Reflect on some past projects where there was a huge feature list. How many of those ideas came to complete fruition? How many of those ideas were really great? Were any of them really duds? I know a lot of mine were!

Detailed plans are useless.

If planning is good, isn't a bigger plan better? There we are, with some vague ideas in mind, which may or may not be things anyone would ever want. But for some reason, we feel that we need to figure out how long each one will take so that we can add them up and decide what will be done a hundred days from Tuesday.

We've all read the horrible statistics about how many software projects go far beyond their budget. Maybe software people are terrible at estimating, and they should try harder. Well, yes, software people are terrible at estimating, because humans are terrible at estimating. Let's not just try harder. Let's find a better way.

Here's a better way: set a time and money budget; produce the most valuable features first; keep the product ready to ship at any time—and stop when the clock runs out. Quite likely we'll even stop before the deadline, because we've already got the important stuff done. We deliver the bulk of the value in far less time, for far less money.

How much long-term detail do you need to set a budget for your project? Is it better to plan for everything, trying to fit it inside the budget? Might it be better to set a tight deadline and build the best possible thing in that time?

Getting started

Ideally, we would begin just by beginning. Get an idea, think about it a bit, put together a little team, and start building. That will tell us quickly whether we can produce something of value, and about how long it will take. Then we can decide to cut our investment, to keep going, or to invest more.

Sometimes our organization just doesn't work that way. They insist on knowing whether this proposed project will take weeks, months, or years, long before they'll decide to invest in it. We might be able to respond by asking to form a team and build for a while. If we can, that's probably the way to go: we can learn a lot quickly. Sometimes that approach, sensible though it is, just won't fly. We need a way to get an initial cut at project size.

A lot has been written about how to do estimation. Yet projects continue to deliver too little, too late. Search for better estimates if you must: I'd prefer to work from a budget, a deadline, a Product Champion who decides what to do next, and a team who can ship software at will.

How much do "they" need to know about a proposed project? How close do we need to be to correct when we bid on it? Can we steer to success within a rough estimate?

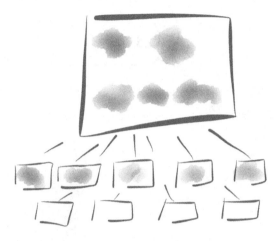

Continuous planning: feature splitting

It's not good enough to plan just at the beginning. Because we're focused on value, we need to plan all the time. The team should be working to a fixed cadence, often called iterations, or *sprints*, a couple of weeks long. Things go best if each feature, often called a *story*, takes only two or three days to do.

I don't recommend working with larger stories and breaking them down into technical items, often called *tasks*. If we use tasks, the business-side people do not have a clear look at how things are going, and they often do not get a good sense of how to help until the end of the two-week sprint interval. Stick with stories: they work better all around.

It's better to break down stories into smaller *stories*, each making sense to the business-side people. As far as I can see, this is always possible. It's a bit tricky at first, but with only a few hours of practice, teams quickly learn how to split features into smaller features, rather than into technical steps.

Think of some big feature that your product needs. How might it be broken down into smaller things? Are some of those things substantially more valuable than others? What does that suggest to you?

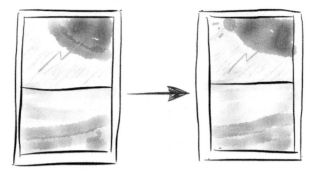

How much work should the team take on?

The answer to this one is clear: the team itself should decide how much work it can accomplish in the next two-week interval. They know better than anyone else, and they will feel more commitment if they make the determination on their own. There are many practices to help the team choose how much to do. They are all based on an idea that I first learned from Kent Beck and Martin Fowler: "Yesterday's Weather."

You'll probably get as much done today as you did yesterday. In iterative projects, plan to do as much this iteration as you did last iteration.

We plan each iteration right before it begins. To decide how much work to take on, we need to understand the work. As a team, we discuss the work. The team's Product Champion presents one feature at a time, followed by a brief team discussion about what it'll take to accomplish the feature. Everyone stays engaged, and the team understands the feature before committing to do it.

I don't recommend estimating the individual work pieces at all. Instead, understand them, and then look at the aggregate and decide how much of it the team can do. If estimates really help the team, go for it. But be careful! The point isn't to make good estimates—the point is to do good work at a consistent pace.

Estimation is risky!

There are some serious risks to estimates: we have an almost irresistible desire to "improve" them, or to compare them. Both of these practices are pernicious. Keep in mind that business and management get the best results by selecting the work to be done and the work to be deferred. Focusing on estimates detracts from this responsibility and is almost certain to create conservative estimates in the hope of creating accurate ones.

Many teams today are working quite successfully using no detailed estimates at all. They think about the work. They break it down, often all the way down to a single test's worth of story. Then they just get to work. When they need to predict how long things will take, they just count things done.

Examine your desire to know estimates and actuals. What would better estimates give you? Which of those things might get in the way of managing scope? Which of those things might be accomplished better by managing scope rather than improving estimates?

Would you prefer to have better estimates if it meant they would be more conservative? Is prediction better than steering?

Planning with "stretch goals" is destructive.

During planning, especially short-term planning, it's tempting to set up "stretch goals" or to "encourage" the team to do "just one more feature." Please do not do this. It's devastatingly destructive. The reason is that the team will in fact try. Eager to please, they'll unconsciously hurry. They'll leave out just a few tests. They'll leave the code not quite as clean as they might have, just to squeeze in one more feature.

Hurrying, they'll inject more defects. Since defects take longer to fix than they do to prevent, hurrying will slow you down. Worse yet, it will slow you down when you least need it, the closer you get to the end of the project.

Dirty code slows you down as well. If the code is clean, the next features go in smoothly. If it gets dirty, everything takes just a bit longer.

Pressure is destructive. Avoid it.

What are some bad things that pressure has caused in your projects? Has it ever increased your defect count? Cost you time? Cost you valuable people? When has pressure really been helpful? Can you think of other ways to get those benefits?

Working without estimates

Once we become proficient at breaking all features down to approximately the same size, we can manage the project very nicely, because we have a good sense of how long things will take. Since our job is to select the work to do versus the work to defer, and to select the most valuable work first, we can steer the project to success without the overhead of estimation.

Estimates remain a controversial topic in software development today. Many people think that estimates and detailed planning are important. Certainly some companies want these things badly, and that may be enough to cause us to do them. Unfortunately, "badly" is almost always how we do with estimates. For teams in flight, estimation is at most an internal matter and may well be almost entirely waste.

Generally speaking, estimates are likely to be wrong, and they focus our attention on the cost of things rather than on value. Consider de-emphasizing or eliminating cost estimates and steering to success by a focus on value.

Plan often, select what's next, don't overeat.

As the project proceeds, we plan every couple of weeks, we decide what the next most important things are to do, and the team decides how many of them to take on. Choose the most valuable ideas first—that's how we grow value most rapidly.

Even over the two-week period of the typical cadence, expect to learn. Sometimes we'll have been too conservative and can pick up a bit more work toward the end. Often, we'll have been too optimistic, or under a bit of pressure, and we'll have taken on too much.

When there's too much food on your plate, don't eat it. That way lies obesity and lethargy. We can't work well with fat, tired code. It's far better to do eight things well than ten things poorly. As soon as you realize the team has taken on too much, remove something from their plate. We're in this for the whole project, and staying healthy is critical.

Further reading:

- Chapter 15, *The "Five-Card Method" for Initial Forecasting*, on page 98.

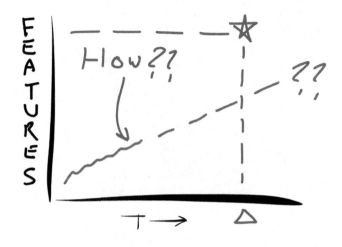

CHAPTER 6

Building the Product, Feature by Feature

Working feature by feature delivers better value. Because the team can show us the software, it's easy to manage and plan. But is this a practical approach? Can our developers really build software feature by feature?

Absolutely! Feature-by-feature development is quite possible. Teams have been doing it successfully for decades. Hundreds of organizations have learned how. Every kind of software that you can imagine is being built feature by feature right now—yes, even the kind of software that you build.

You and your organization can benefit from the feature-by-feature approach. Everyone needs to learn a bit, and change a bit. Improved management and faster return makes it worthwhile.

Let's take a quick look at what's required to work feature by feature, and then drill into some details.

If we want small features frequently, what, in general, will all of us need to do? What specific pitfalls do you see?

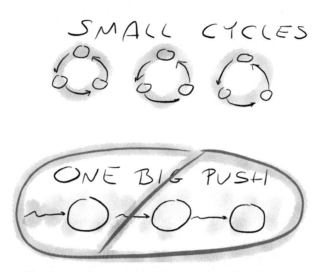

Build a tiny product, completely, in each small cycle.

We plan and manage our project in short one- or two-week cycles. In each cycle, we define the next few features to build and we say how they'll be tested. The team then builds the features and we all verify whether they pass the tests.

In each of these one- or two-week iterations, we go through a complete product development cycle, from concept to ready to ship. At first we may not be very good at it, but in a few iterations we'll begin to get the process shaken down. At that point we'll have an increasingly predictable series of subsets of the project, each one cleaner, and more ready to go, than the last.

In each cycle, we learn. We learn how much we can do in a couple of weeks. We learn how to test whether we have done what we set out to do. We learn the most effective way to define features without excess overhead. We learn how to build feature by feature while keeping the code and design clear and alive.

What difficulties can you foresee if you begin to build complete versions of the product in small cycles? What could go wrong? What will you have to learn?

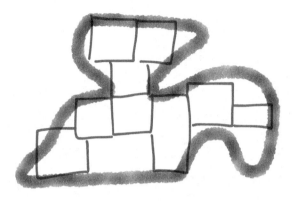

Refine the product vision.

In a feature-by-feature approach, we ask the development team to build features every couple of weeks. We want to see things coming out that we actually want, not some technical whatnot that we don't understand.

This means that our business-side people need to build up skill in breaking down large, vague, sweeping requirements into small, practical next steps that deliver maximum value for minimum effort. They'll need help from around the organization, and perhaps from outside, to get good at this. Mostly, they need to work at it: trust them and their teams to figure out what they need.

This is no small task, but it's critical to success. We need to sharpen our vision of what the product must do—and what's just "nice to have." The result is a faster return on our software investment.

What big features have you in mind for your product? What small pieces can you identify that would help you see how you're doing and what to do next? What software should we show you, right now?

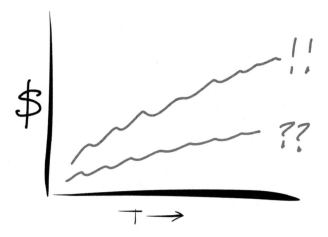

Always work on the highest possible value next.

As we progress through the iterations, it becomes increasingly clear how much work we can finish by "the date." It's critical to do the most valuable features first. The team works together to identify the high-value, low-cost features we can do. The team learns to build the best possible product within the time and money available.

We must do all this in the open. Everyone needs to see the actual progress. We can't accept "90 percent done." Features need to be "done" or "not done": there is no middle ground. We have to see what's going on inside the project so that we can guide it to the best possible conclusion.

What do we need to know about each feature as it gets "done"? What could interfere with our ability to guide the project and grow the product?

Identify real progress.

The feature-by-feature style includes a complete development cycle in every iteration: requirements, design, coding, and testing. They are all present all the time so that they're all visible all the time. Feature-by-feature development is safe, practical, and effective. It will work for you.

As our project goes on, we'll be learning how to tell the difference between apparent progress and real progress. We'll be building up an understanding of when "done" really means done in our unique situation.

When we can see real, running features, we have clear and solid information about our project's condition. When we're not able to look at features, or they aren't done, we won't know what's going on.

When your team starts building features and telling you they're done, what might make those glowing reports misleadingly optimistic? How can they be made more accurate?

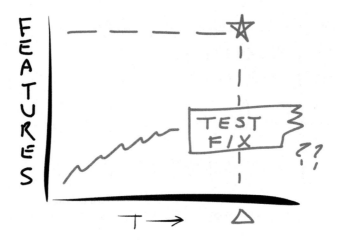

Eliminate the test-and-fix finish.

Many projects end with a test-and-fix interval that seems to drag on forever, furrowing into our soul. This can even happen when we work feature by feature—if the features aren't really done.

Because we're learning to complete each one- or two-week iteration with finished, potentially shippable software, we are learning how to reduce or eliminate that long unknown block of test and fix time that shows up at the end of so many projects.

For feature-by-feature development to work, the software needs to be nearly free of defects at the end of every two-week iteration. It needs to be nearly free of defects all the time.

To be sure we're free of defects, we need to check everything, all the time. That's not as hard as you think; we'll talk more about it later. But first, there's more!

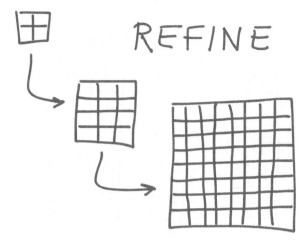

Grow and refine the design as we go.

As we build feature by feature, being free of defects isn't enough. We also need to grow the design as we go. If we design too much, we won't get as many features, and that will show up. If we design too little, features will be hard to do, we'll slow down, and again that will become visible.

By observing how our velocity—the pace at which we ship features—changes, we'll learn how to "right-size" our design effort. Too much design, we slow down. Too little, we slow down. Tweak, observe, tweak again.

This is a tricky area. Most of us have seen software whose design got so bad that progress became almost impossible. The techniques for keeping the design good enough are easy to learn. They are also easy to forget, especially if we put teams under enough pressure.

How can we help our developers keep the design clean? Do they have the needed skills? What should we avoid that would discourage clean design?

Further reading:

- Chapter 18, *To Speed Up, Build with Skill,* on page 116
- Chapter 19, *Refactoring,* on page 120

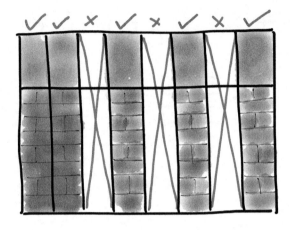

Our product needs a solid foundation.

CHAPTER 7

Build Features and Foundation in Parallel

Every product has a set of key features needed to deliver value. We plan to build those and X out the rest.

Everything we build must rest on a solid foundation. We often use words like *architecture, design,* or *infrastructure* when talking about the foundation.

According to the guidance in this book, we're going to build those features incrementally, starting with the most valuable, down to the least valuable. To keep the features coming smoothly, we need to keep the system's design solid from the first day to the last.

How can we best balance design and features as we go along?

Each feature needs a solid foundation of design, a solid "infrastructure."

Without a good design foundation, the product will be full of defects and hard to work with. We will slow down and quite possibly fail. There's no disputing this: features do need to be supported by a foundation, and the foundation needs to be well designed.

We can't build features without a foundation. What's the best way to approach building features, given that we require a solid foundation?

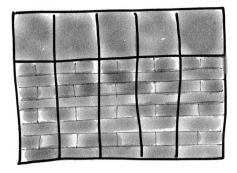

Ideally we would deliver all the features, complete, by the deadline.

Remember that when we envisioned all these features, we imagined everything we might want if we could have it all. It's very unlikely that we'll get everything we want.

Even after prioritizing, we surely have too much to do! We need to do as little work as possible to deliver the best possible product by our delivery date...and we need to do that work as soundly as we can afford.

We need to build features and foundation in a way that will keep us safe, keep us moving rapidly, and waste as little time and effort as possible. Let's consider some options: We could build out the whole design first, or we could build each full feature one at a time, each with its foundation. Both of these approaches raise concerns.

Foundation first means too few features get to market.

If we build out the design first, we almost always wind up with too few shippable features by the date!

We're not sure how fast we can go: we never are. If we build foundation first, we will surely build too much of it. We'll consume too much time and we'll wind up with fewer features than we could have had.

Each feature represents value to our users, and revenue or other benefits to us. We need as many as we can reasonably get.

Even if we do have time to do all the foundation and then build the features on top, we can guide our project only when we can see the actual working features created. Building foundation first inhibits our ability to manage our work.

We dare not build the foundation first: it will defer and inevitably reduce the product's value.

Well then, what about building up each feature, each with its foundation, one at a time?

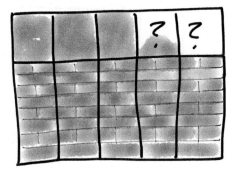

Building complete features one at a time still means too few features get to market.

If we build complete features one after another, we're likely to have key capabilities missing when time runs out.

When we envision a major feature, we see it in its fullest possible glory, just as we see our product with every possible feature.

Just as it would be wrong to build every possible feature, it is wrong to start by building each feature out to its fullest glory. The desirability of our product depends on a set of features that is complete enough—and glorious enough—to attract and satisfy our users.

What's left? We can't build all the foundation first, and we can't build all the features first. Are we doomed?

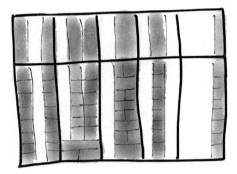

Build simple yet functional versions first.

It's safer by far to build a simple yet functional version of each feature first!

To get the best product in the time available, we need to work on all the features that are important to our users, not just a few. For each feature, we need to fill in as much capability as time permits, using our judgment as to what's needed and how much time we have left.

We can do the best possible job of this if we do small versions of each necessary feature, with just enough foundation to be solid.

We build what's called a "minimum viable product" as quickly as we can.

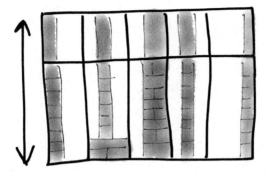

Refine each feature in multiple iterations.

We fill in the features smoothly, always with our best judgment of what's most important, building just enough infrastructure as we go.

Rather than take chances with how much infrastructure to build, or how many features we will be able to get done by our finish date, we work in small versions. Each feature version makes the product a bit better so that we always have the best possible product at every moment.

We can repeat this in every iteration, making priority decisions as we go, until time and money tell us that it's time to stop or switch attention to a new product, as discussed in Chapter 2, *Value Is What We Want*, on page 6.

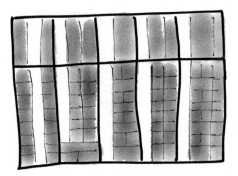

Steer to the best possible result by the desired shipping date.

Because we have the best possible product at every moment, we have the best possible product at the moment we decide to ship it. In fact, because we're always ready, we can ship early if there is any reason to do so—and there often is!

This does take skill!

Choosing the best mix of features requires great skill on the part of our Product Champion. This skill can be developed, however, and the repeated pqractice of choosing the features for the next iteration is the best way to develop that skill. An engaged Product Champion sees her vision for the product coming into being and learns to make better choices by practicing choosing often.

The developers need skill as well. Developers are often trained to try to design a system up front. As we see here, this is never ideal, because we never know up front what the system will be. This is especially true when our Product Champion is learning what she wants, what she can have, and how to grow the best possible system.

What are the skills that our whole team needs in order to work this way? What guidance must the business-side people provide? How can we help our technical people do their part?

Build walls against bugs using good processes.

CHAPTER 8

Bug-Free and Well Designed

Good technical practices are required to ensure that our product is bug-free and well designed at all times. What are they?

Let's look in a bit more detail at what developers must do in order to work feature by feature. Don't worry—we're not going to drop into programming—but we do want all our readers to be aware of what the business needs to expect of developers, and what it needs to support.

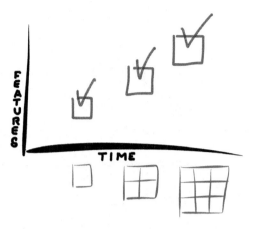

Our product is made up of a growing set of correctly working features, built on a growing, evolving foundation of design.

We're asking our team to build feature by feature, keeping everything checked and working, in good order, improving the design as they go. This is our best chance to steer the project to success. But there are issues.

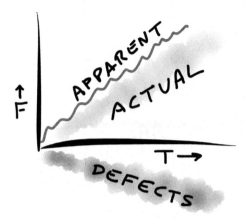

Defects amount to negative features. Progress is uncertain. Eliminate defects to provide clarity on what's done.

We're trying to plan by features, grow by features, and manage by features. This means that when we're told a feature is done, it really needs to work. Any defects in our features amount to negative features. They reduce our line of apparent progress. If the defects aren't discovered yet, it's even worse: we don't even know how bad things are.

We cannot work effectively in a world of defects.

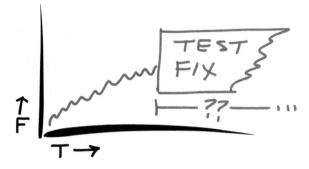

Defect repair adds unknown delay. Repair as you go to provide clarity on what's done.

As consultant Tom DeMarco tells us, no one sees a roach on the floor of a restaurant and says "There goes the roach." It's the same with bugs—that is, with defects. Where there's one, there are likely many.

Finding defects takes time. Fixing them takes time. If we leave this until the end of the project, our plans for new features will be disrupted, and we will still have to decide which defects to leave in the system.

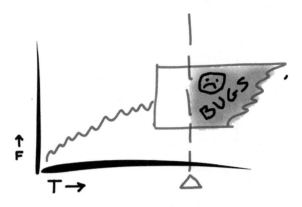

If we don't know in time what's done, and how well it's done, we'll have no choice but to ship late with visible defects. That's bad business.

"Bug triage?" No, thanks. We need to prevent as many defects as we can, because they add unknown delay right at the end of our project. We look like fools for shipping late, and we look like fools for shipping buggy software. Let's not go there.

Because features are being added and enhanced, and because the design is evolving, we will make mistakes. We need continuous comprehensive testing.

There's really no way out. At the end of every iteration, we need to have the software as close to defect-free as possible. The only way to get there is to test it.

Because we're growing the system all the time, we need to test it more and more, better and better. We need to test the new features, but we need to check the old ones as well, to make sure they haven't been broken.

We test at two levels, with "Business" tests and "Programmer" tests.

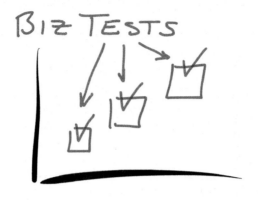

At the end of every iteration, we need business-level tests to verify that we have received what we asked for.

We're getting new features every two weeks. We need to know whether the new ones work, and we need to be sure that old ones haven't broken. To accomplish this, we must build business-level tests and checks for every aspect of every feature that we possibly can.

If we don't check something, we don't know whether it works. We have to check everything. The testing burden will grow with each new feature. We have to keep up with this burden.

The best known way to keep up is to express our features in terms of the tests they must pass, and to automate the tests to give us assurance that the feature works now, and from now on. This is often called *acceptance test-driven development.*

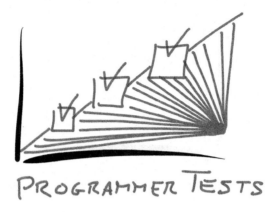

PROGRAMMER TESTS

Developers make changes every day. To ensure they don't waste time, developer tests need to be checked much more frequently.

The creation of a single feature requires hundreds, even thousands of lines of code. Any one of those lines could be wrong, and if it is, something, somewhere, will break.

We could rely on our business-level tests to catch these problems, but they usually take a long time to run, and they don't point to the specific programming error when they do fail. Developers need to build a comprehensive network of automated tests as well, to be sure that problems are found sooner and fixed more readily.

The best way we know to do this is to write the developer tests first, then make them run. This is called *test-driven development*, or *TDD*. TDD's greatest strength is in supporting design improvement, which we'll discuss a bit later.

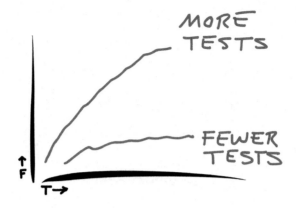

Almost paradoxically, all this testing makes our team go faster! The reason: We make fewer mistakes, and they're found more quickly.

It takes longer to find a problem, and to fix it, than it does to prevent the problem in the first place. When we work with business-level tests, provided with the feature requests, we don't ship the feature until the test runs. When we work with developer-level tests, written before or in conjunction with coding, we don't ship any part of the software until all the tests run.

Testing as part of our ongoing work prevents defects from getting into the program. This lets us go much faster than we would if we coded and only tested when we thought the code was done.

At the beginning, there are only a few small features. The design can be simple.

Remember, we're working incrementally. We're shipping *real working features* every two weeks. We need a good design early on, but we only need a small good design.

The design can easily deteriorate.

As we add software, even to a good design, things tend to get worse. We hammer this here, bend that there. Good designs go bad one decision at a time. We can prevent this, but we must work skillfully and fix it as we go.

Inferior design will slow us down. Skill and care are required to keep our project alive.

As the system grows feature by feature, the design needs to grow.

We need to have a good design at all times. A bad design slows us down, because it is hard to change. As the project grows, as the features grow, we must grow the design to support those features. We need a high-quality design at every moment.

At each stage of feature building, the team must do enough design improvement to keep up.

Every change tends to break our current design. To keep the design good, we need to improve it as we go. Perhaps we make a nice clean space for our new feature. Perhaps we push the feature in and then rearrange things to get a good design. Either way works. What doesn't work is to let the design go.

Keeping the design good as it changes is called *refactoring*. Refactoring is a necessary skill for this way of developing software. We'll talk more about refactoring elsewhere. For now, let's focus on what it's good for.

Failure to keep the design good enough will slow progress, or even stop it!

If our design is allowed to deteriorate, progress will slow. Features will cost more than they should. Unless we keep the design fresh, we'll just get slower and slower.

Testing and refactoring work together to make feature-by-feature development possible. The nature of the work requires us to test and refactor. There is no better way known today.

Business needs to know that the program works. *Acceptance test-driven development* is one good way to keep current on what's working. Developers need to know precisely what's broken when something breaks. *Test-driven development* is a key tool in accomplishing that. A strong suite of automated tests keeps us certain that things work, and having two layers of test, a Business layer and a Developer layer, works best.

To progress, the design must improve continually. Improving the design by refactoring is the technique for doing this. But even the best refactoring can break something. Our business-side and technical-side test suites give us the confidence to do the design improvement that we need to do.

For the best quality, smoothest progress, and greatest predictability, this is the best known way to work. Testing and refactoring are critical tools in feature-by-feature development. Don't leave home without them.

Further reading:

- Chapter 18, *To Speed Up, Build with Skill*, on page 116

- Chapter 19, *Refactoring*, on page 120

- Chapter 14, *Creating Teams That Thrive*, on page 94

- Chapter 17, *Whip the Ponies Harder*, on page 112

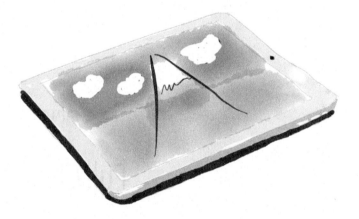

Let me explain. No, there is too much. Let me sum up.

CHAPTER 9

Full Circle

1. Value is what we want. Features deliver value. Delivering features early gives us value sooner.

2. Managing by looking at value works better than managing by dates or artifacts that don't deliver value.

3. Planning features is easy enough to do. Estimate if you must. Selecting the work based on Yesterday's Weather works better.

4. Building by features requires us to build a small, complete product, every couple of weeks. That product must always work correctly, and it must always be well designed.

5. Development must deliver real working features. The product must be well tested. Business-side people and developers contribute to testing. The product must be well designed. Developers keep the design alive all the time.

That's all there is to it. Very simple. A commitment from the top of the business, down to the individual managers and developers, is all it takes. Let's get going! Show me the software!

Further reading:

- Chapter 13, *Not That Simple,* on page 92

Part II

Notes and Essays

The essential flow of software development is simple, as we've discussed in Part I. Good work is simple; it is not easy. The details, of course, are endless. In this part we take a closer look at a few of those details. Here you'll find short notes and essays on topics that interest me—and, I hope, you!

CHAPTER 10

Value—What Is It?

A reader asked: "Ron, in Chapter 2, Value Is What We Want, on page 6, you just say that value is what we want. Isn't that an oversimplification?"

I replied: "Well, yes, as is everything in this book." Let me say a few more words, however, to help out a bit. See also Chapter 11, Value—How Can We Measure It?, on page 84.

In the book Zen and the Art of Motorcycle Maintenance [Pir00], Robert Pirsig's protagonist, Phaedrus, is exploring the idea of quality. At one point he reaches the statement: "Quality is what you like." I'm offering a similar thought here.

In Agile software development—as in many other realms—we talk about the notion of value. We make decisions about what to do, or what not to do, based on value. We do things sooner if they are of higher value, and we do things later if their value is lower. What do we mean by value?

Value is, simply, "what you want."

You may at first feel that this statement is too Zen, or that it has no meaning at all. Let's explore here what we might mean by value, and how we work with it. My aim is to help you see that value is in fact, what you want, what you care about.

Agile methods ask us to choose the order in which we do things based on value. Sometimes we might say *business value* or *customer value,* as if these qualifications help. In a way, they do help, because they may cause us to think about things we value in terms of "good for the business" or "good for the customer." But these are far from the only kinds of value we might consider. Let's look at just a few more.

We might be choosing a strategic direction for our product. We decide that we need information about what users would prefer, so we create some prototypes and show them to potential users.

We value information.

Our product might be aimed at saving lives; perhaps it helps us ship vaccines around the world quickly. We decide to choose our next features based on the number of lives saved by those features.

We value human life.

Our company might be running out of cash. We decide to get some venture capital and to produce a sample product quickly to show to would-be investors.

We value capital. We value company survival. We value the ability to help the customers we may someday have if we stay in business.

Our product might be too slow. Customers are using alternatives because they do not like the speed of our product. We decide to defer features to speed up the software.

We value product speed.

Our progress might be too slow, taking too long to get things done. We decide to defer features to clean up the software so that we can develop faster.

We value rapid progress.

Our product might display funny cat pictures. Our purpose might be to make people smile, to provide a bit of happiness in their day.

We value people's happiness.

We value joy. We value creativity. We value collaboration. We value money. We value revenue. We value the ability to keep working. We value the ability to be with people we care about, doing things we care about. We value human life, or even kitty life.

These are just a few of the things that make up value. The problem of the "Product Owner," of management, of all the people who decide what we should do next, is to look deeply at the many things we value, and to choose a sequence of development that gives us the best possible result in return for our time, money, and effort in building our product.

It would be nice if it were easier. It would be nice if we could just say "Value is revenue over the next 90 days," or "Value is what the VP of Sales wants." It might even work for some people, some companies, sometimes. But no such definition will work for everyone, and in my opinion, it won't work very well for anyone. If we are to survive as a company or as individuals, we need to look deeply at value, and to choose the things that matter, among all the things we might do.

Choosing value is choosing what matters to you.

Value…is what you want.

CHAPTER 11

Value—How Can We Measure It?

We began by suggesting that "Value is what you want" and advising you to produce small bits of real value every couple of weeks. We asked you to say "Show us the software" to see what's really going on. The main idea is to concentrate on value, not cost, and to see that value in terms of real, running software with features we can understand.

But Ron, you talk about value as if it's purely subjective. Shouldn't we be using real, solid numerical information to make our decisions? What do you have against measurement?

Well, it's a fair cop: I am pushing back against using numerical measures, in value and even in cost estimates. There are some reasons for this.

We don't really know the numbers.

For almost any product of interest, we don't know the numbers. We don't know how many users will use our feature. We don't know how many lives will be saved. We don't know if people will rate our latest idea with three stars or five. We don't know if people will buy our product based on this idea, or refuse to buy it.

Big differences are important; small ones aren't.

When we look at all the feature options before us, some of them are incredibly important, and some are really dull and boring. That's the distinction that matters: what's incredibly important versus what's boring.

Different kinds of value aren't comparable.

A Product Champion values many different things. The values go up and down as time goes on. Sometimes we need customer information: will people find this idea useful? Sometimes we need development information: will this idea take a day to do, a week, or ten years? Sometimes we value pleasing some customer or prospect: if we can give them this feature quickly, they'll give us their money. *Then what should we do?*

But Ron, then what is "value"? How should we measure it? How will we know we have it?

Don't panic! You already have a very good idea what value is. Take any two things you might do. Ask yourself which one to do next—which one is more valuable right now. It turns out you almost always know. If you don't know, ask yourself whether either one of them is worth doing at all. Often, you'll find they're not.

Then ask yourself *why* you prefer what you prefer. Write down a few notes. Ask again: *why*. This will give you a sense of some of the dimensions of value to you. Ask your stakeholders. Whether they agree with you or not, ask why. Build up a grasp of what's important, and why.

It's always tempting to try to express value in numbers, and if you have a way to do that, go ahead and use it. Then look at two things your numbers suggest and ask yourself whether you agree. If you do, go ahead. If not, that's interesting! Dig into that until you and your numbers agree. If they just won't, I'd advise throwing out the numbers.

Looking for numbers puts us on a bit of a slippery slope. If the company's purpose with the product is to make money, then we could measure the product by how much money is made. But there's no useful way to know whether that number is a good measure of anything, since it conflates sales concerns, product concerns, and of course, customer concerns.

Even worse, most monetary measures are trailing indicators: we don't get information until it's too late. We have no real way of knowing whether the revenue number is really good or really bad. Money is a terrible indicator: too slow, unclear when we get it.

I wish I had an easy answer, like counting up function points or user preference clicks or the like. Use those if you find them valuable, but know that the true value of all the measures you can think of is to build up an understanding, in your Product Champion, your stakeholders, and your team, about what's really valuable.

Instead, sit with your developers and stakeholders. Consider the things you might do. Select a combination of next things to do that the group agrees is most valuable. The true value in doing this is the learning that will come from reaching a consensus.

Then build it, ship it promptly, and listen to your users. Repeat.

CHAPTER 12

Of Course It's Hard!

Early readers of this book have said, "Ron, you make this seem clear and simple and compelling. We should focus on value, plan by value, manage by value, and build by value. That's all very well and good. But software development is hard! It's very hard!"

Of course it's hard. It's the nature of what we're doing that we're always pushing our own limits. The point of this book, however, is that the approach we should take to doing these hard things is to insist: "Show us the software!" That lets us accomplish the following:

- Focus on what we value, so we can get the best results.

- Produce real software often so that we can learn what we want.

- Build what we want in small steps, so we can see how we're doing.

- Learn the planning, management, and technical skills that we need, so we can build the product rapidly and well.

Every aspect of this work is complex, but we do not need a complex process to do the work. A complex process holds us back, imposing rote activity when we need to observe what's going on, adjust it, and improve it.

We do need increasing skill, which we can guide best by using a simple process aimed at delivering value.

You will have to decide specifically "how" to do these things. The point of this book is to help you improve your intuition about how. There are no fixed "best" ways, so even if you decide to do some specific thing for a while, keep checking that it's really helping. You will need to change things.

Take every idea as, maybe, a good way to start doing things for a while. Then make the process your own, and build your own ideas. But keep it simple!

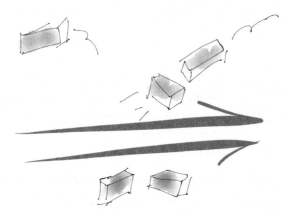

It's still difficult, Ron!

Yes, but it gets better.

Doing the work in this way results in rapid improvement. As a team we repeatedly decide what to do, then do it, then inspect the result. The problems are always hard; building good software is always hard. But the team becomes more powerful and thus progresses faster.

When I had my knee replaced (long story), I could barely walk at first. A few meters caused me pain, and after the pain was gone, I was still not strong enough to walk very far. I kept trying, kept walking, and it got to be less painful. I was able to go much farther. Today, I can still walk far enough to make myself tired, but it's no longer a matter of a few feet.

It's the same with this cyclical development process. At first, it hurts and we don't get much done. After a little while, we get a lot more done, and it doesn't hurt as much. And it's a good kind of hurt, not the kind that tells you you've damaged something.

I wish I had better news. The fact is that it's not easy to be excellent. However, you can be as good as you care to be, simply by continuing to work and continuing to improve how you work.

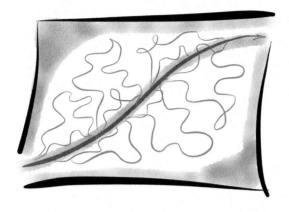

CHAPTER 13

Not That Simple

Ron, it's not that simple. Do you think I'm a fool? —Early
reviewer, paraphrased.

Of course it's not that simple. We need to recognize that often it can be nearly this simple, and always, we wish it could be.

As we wander the twisty little passages, all different, let's keep in mind that we're trying to follow this simple ideal path, focusing on value, managing and planning by value, building valuable things, and observing them to see what's going on.

Things will get hairy while we do that. All the complications of real business will show up. All the complications that we seem to throw in our own way will show up.

And yet, it's all about deciding what we want, guiding ourselves toward what we really want, by building things and seeing how they work out.

Purpose, Autonomy, Mastery

CHAPTER 14

Creating Teams That Thrive

Many of us, when managing something, feel the need to provide a lot of direction. But in this book, I ask you to ensure that your teams know *what* to do and to let them figure out *how*. How could this possibly work?

In his book *Drive [Pin09]*, Daniel Pink speaks of Purpose, Autonomy, and Mastery as drivers of both employee satisfaction and improved productivity. These ideas resonate with me, and make a lot of sense in the context of the Natural Way. Let's explore.

Purpose comes from the business.

A dedicated business-side person is needed to guide your development team by identifying what's to be done and what's to be deferred. This designated person is sometimes called the Product Owner, or the Customer. In this book I use the term Product Champion, because the best results come when the whole team feels ownership in the product, with one business-side person providing vision and "championing" the product.

The Product Champion provides purpose, both broadly and in detail, and keeps in daily contact with your team, ensuring that they understand why the effort exists, what the most important issues are, and how the product can best serve those issues. Bring concerns or problems to the team, and let the whole team create solutions in concert.

In some teams, the Product Champion brings in defined solutions rather than concerns or problems. This can work but it's far from ideal. Your team will be slower to gain a sense of purpose if they are spoon-fed solutions rather than being allowed to creatively solve problems.

When the whole team works together on problems, the Product Champion learns better what she wants and how to express it. The whole team improves, and so does the Champion. This is the sweet spot.

Autonomy gives the team responsibility.

The Product Champion shows *what problem to solve;* the team decides *how to solve it.* With true autonomy, no one double-checks the team: they decide, they build, we all see the results. Everyone learns.

As a team, in each two-week iteration, let's confer with our Product Champion on what needs to be done. Select a quantity of work that we can deliver in good order, figure out how to do it, then self-organize to get it done. Then, "Show us the software."

As our team becomes self-organizing, we'll have more autonomy, bring more creativity to the problem, and become more productive.

A self-organizing team with a common understanding of its purpose: this is the sweet spot.

Mastery comes from the iterative process.

In each iteration, our team works to produce a "done" increment of software. At first we will have difficulty, but in each iteration, we meet and look back on how things went and determine how to do better. We move toward mastery.

In each iteration, let's improve our definition of "done," the criteria by which an increment will be considered to be good enough. Make it more mature and stringent. Move as a team toward mastery.

Each iteration constitutes practice in producing "done" software. It ends with "Show us the software," enabling everyone to see how good it is, and to contribute to working out how to make it better. Again, they move toward mastery.

The mantra of Scrum, the most popular Agile method, is "Inspect and Adapt." As a team, we observe what we accomplish, note what's holding us back, and improve the situation. As the team improves, we all move toward mastery.

Summing Up

A masterful self-organizing team with a common understanding of its purpose.

This is the sweet spot.

CHAPTER 15

The "Five-Card Method" for Initial Forecasting

If we simply must do initial large-scale forecasting, we can use the "Five-Card Method" to get just enough detail but not too much. We take our grand vision and break each component down into elements small enough for our team members to feel that they know what it means and that they can build it in a week:

- Consider the three to five most important "epics"—the big things that describe the product you have in mind. On a card, describe each one in a single sentence.

- Break down each of these into three to five smaller cards. Make each one more specific and clear—and, of course, smaller. Make sure that each item makes business sense: it should be a "feature," not some technical idea or widget.

- Repeat the breakdown until each feature seems to be about the same size. What's a good size? Something the team members think they can build in about a week. That's small enough. * As you break things down, keep a close eye out for things that bear high value and things that don't. Set low-value things aside. Remember that you're going to make the date, not by whipping the ponies harder (as we've discussed in Chapter 17, *Whip the Ponies Harder*, on page 112), but by managing carefully what we do and what we defer until later.

What are the top-level bullet-point features of your product? What are the bullet points for the detailed slide for each of them? What more do you need to know to decide to go ahead?

Directing

Staffing   Planning

Controlling   Organizing

CHAPTER 16

Managing Natural Software Development

Someone said to me, "Ron, in the real world there are managers. They're there for a reason. In your model you don't say much about them. What about managers?"

Well, I like to think that we're in the business of creating the "real world," not putting up with it. Management does need to happen. It turns out, it doesn't need to be "management as usual." Let's explore.

When we work in the Natural Way, much of the "managing" is done inside the team. The Product Champion sets the vision and, working with stakeholders and team members, sets the priorities. The team "shows us the software" every couple of weeks so that everyone can tell how things are going. This lets us coordinate with stakeholders outside the team and allows us to easily judge whether the team needs help of some kind.

The team is fully cross-functional and has all the skills and capacity needed to deliver each increment of software. Team members do their own testing, their own documentation, everything. The closer we get to this ideal, the less coordination we need.

The team is self-organizing as well. Team members decide how to parcel out the work, and then ensure that it gets done well. When teams are working as described here, they require very little ongoing management.

Management work still needs to be done, of course. Staffing *selections* should be made by the team to the highest degree possible. However, staffing *decisions*, whether to hire or fire, need to be made by management. Budget proposals might be made by the team together with the Product Champion. Budget decisions, within and across projects, are a management function.

Managers sometimes wonder whether they'll work themselves out of a job by letting go of so much of their work. But think about it. In management, this is called "delegation." If a manager creates an effective team, building a valuable product, visibly and smoothly, that manager is going to get more to do, not less. Build another team, and another.

Let's consider Peter Drucker's components of management: planning, organizing, staffing, directing, and controlling. We'll look at each of these, and what these ideas mean for managers, in the context of the Natural Way.

Ron, getting beyond "management as usual" sounds fine, but I work for a company that has long-term goals and I can assure you we have a need for longer-term planning. How do you suggest we approach that?

Somewhere "upward" in the company, management decides what the business of the organization is. They decide in general terms what will be done, and who will do it. This begins with an overall planning activity, selecting the suite of problems to be solved and opportunities to be undertaken, and determining the size of each of those efforts in terms of time, staffing, and budget.

From the viewpoint of the Natural Way, long-term planning can be done in nearly any way at all. People from all disciplines should be involved in this activity: management people, finance people, product people, technical people.

Probably the most important thing to do from the top? Limit the number of products and programs you take on. Get those done, and then add more. Working on lots of things in parallel just slows everything down.

What about planning at the scale of a few months or a year?

A medium- or long-term effort starts out with fairly general goals. Following the Natural Way, we build high-value features early, and managers can keep an eye on where we are without obsessing over details. As high-level planners and managers, let's be clear on the general capabilities needed in our large project, and let's ask our Product Champions to "show us the software" that provides those capabilities. Let's help our Champions cover all the key aspects of the product first and then fill in the less important aspects as time and money permit.

What about short-term planning, day to day, week to week?

In the Natural Way, short-term planning is continuous at the level of development. Valuable features are given priorities, and they get done in the order of highest value first. Week in and week out, value grows visibly. The plan is revised every couple of weeks and we can all see how things are going.

We do this very simply. Every couple of weeks, we observe what has been accomplished and we plan the next couple of weeks, keeping our eye on the overall vision and goals for our effort.

My experience has been that managing is mostly about trying to keep projects on track. How do we ensure that we are keeping to the plan?

Honestly, our job isn't to stick to the plan—it's to steer our course for the best result, not some fixed target.

When we deploy our products often, delivering real value to our users, we often find that we can stop far before the time and money run out. Why? Because we've already done everything customers really need. We often find that, instead of whatever we imagined the product should be, new ideas have bubbled up. Working in the Natural Way, we steer the project—we don't just plan and then hope.

Always keep an eye on the value. At the planning level, always ask what the most valuable next things are. To track how the plan is going, ask the Product Champion to show us the software, and to relate what it does to the value we're asking for.

Ron, your advice sounds good, but I've often found that it comes down to having the right people in the right positions. How can we best make the necessary organizational decisions?

Upper-level management also has the responsibility for general organization. They allocate money and people to the work. Generally, having determined the budget, management selects the Product Champion and (possibly) some of the personnel. Often, the Product Champion selects the core team members and the team as a whole selects the rest. Within that framework, the Product Champion and team self-organize to get the work done.

Try to push detailed organizational decisions downward as far as possible. Use budgeting to control the size of efforts. Focus on results as much as you can, and allow the people closer to the work to make most of the decisions about what to do and how to organize to do it.

What about staffing decisions? Who decides who should be hired or fired?

Very likely, personnel actions must be initiated or at least approved by management. More and more, however, the choices and recommendations are delegated to the team. Let your teams determine whether they want to add more people, and let them choose who to add. They understand better than you will what they need.

Help the team understand policy issues, overall hiring guidelines and strategies, and most of all, the value of building on the people you already have. The better your teams understand the bigger picture, the better things will go.

Management is supposed to direct what goes on. If all these decisions are being made at the bottom of the organization, how can management provide necessary direction?

Based on long-term planning, management has decided what products and projects to invest in. They have selected a Product Champion who will be accountable for the results of each effort. Management views each product as it comes into being, and supports and guides the Product Champion, making sure they remain aligned with the corporate purpose for the product. Direction takes a few primary forms.

Sometimes things change in the environment or the company's priorities. These changes are passed down in terms of adjustments to product vision, budget, and the like.

Sometimes as managers view the results of the work, they'll discover things that they did not express well or that improve their understanding of what's needed. These, too result in adjustments to the team's vision.

Sometimes things may not go as well as they might. Working as we recommend in this book, management will see deviations promptly and can respond by helping the Product Champion and team to do better. Big surprises should be nearly impossible when you can see the product every couple of weeks.

But work has to be controlled. How do we make sure that, day to day, things are under control?

Day to day, teams control how they do the work. The Product Champion controls, week to week, what they work on. Management observes the results of that work and makes sure that progress is commensurate with the time and money being spent. If deviations exist, management might take action. That action would not be taken by stepping in and doing the work, but by providing assistance and training, and, if need be, by adjusting budgets, staffing, and responsibilities.

Summing Up

The Natural Way of software development calls for delegating authority to the people who do the work. There's nothing new about this; it's how management has always been done. True, some managers have been hesitant to fully delegate for fear of being unable to help if needed. Fortunately, this style of software development provides plenty of visibility into what's going on, which makes delegation quite safe.

When our teams "show us the software," we always know where they are, what they're working on, and how things are going. Follow these guidelines thoughtfully and you'll be in good shape.

CHAPTER 17

Whip the Ponies Harder

A high-level manager was told that a project was moving more slowly than had been hoped. He retorted, "Well, we'll just have to whip the ponies harder."

I find it difficult to think of a management comment more repugnant than that. In addition, it was sure to backfire.

Under pressure, teams give up the wrong things. They don't test enough; they leave the code in poor condition. This reduces value, increases the delay to getting the value, and reduces the value they can deliver later.

Under pressure, teams test less and therefore put more defects in. Some of these defects escape the room and affect customers. Value is directly reduced.

Some defects are discovered before the product ships. This usually means that we have a testing phase that comes after we think we are "done." Already this is delaying delivery of value.

Worse yet, we have to take time to fix the problems. This rework delays and reduces value even more.

Finally, when our teams work under pressure, they leave the code in bad condition. This makes adding new features harder and slows down value delivery even more.

How many defects do you have now? Do you really want more? How often do developers say that the condition of the code slows them down? Did your innocent pressure cause those things?

We need more features! Why can't we just increase velocity?

Frankly, when I look into an organization that "needs more features," what I almost invariably find is an organization that can't say no. They have become order takers rather than decision makers. They're working on some things of value, perhaps, but much of the work they're doing doesn't bring much real value to their products—or to their customers.

No, really we need more features! The programmers have to go faster!

Your programmers are going as fast as they reasonably can. There may be ways that the code can be improved over time so that they can go faster. There are almost certainly ways to reduce defect injection, which saves you all that fixing time. Those are improvements that take time to make, and they cannot be made by a team under pressure.

One way that we can subtly cause pressure, leading to the problems we just talked about, is to ask the team to "increase velocity." This means "get more done." Teams will try to do that. They will do so by turning the invisible dials of quality and estimation.

If they reduce quality, we'll get more defects and go slower. We don't want that.

Under pressure, teams will consciously or unconsciously begin to be more conservative in what they take on. They will begin rating things as a bit larger or a bit harder than they used to. This will give the impression that they're going faster, but they are not.

What would a team need to do, or need to know, in order to produce more work per unit time? Do you believe that "work harder" answers that question? What can management do to help a team be truly more productive?

Are there any ways to go faster? How can we do it?

If you must try to go faster, analyze sources of delay. These usually have more impact than individual productivity.

Work on team productivity before individual productivity. Ensure that each team has a good mix of skills. Make sure that each team has all the skills needed to do the work. Team members with key skills should be full time, not shared. Use specialists to increase other individuals' abilities. Value working together.

Increase individual productivity by increasing capability, not by urging people to work harder. "Work smarter, not harder" means that we have to help them get smarter.

What are the real causes of delay on your project? Is decision making slowing you down? Defect correction? Handing things off between individuals or teams? What's your delay? Work on that.

Can we at least use our velocity to predict when we'll be done?

In a word, no! We do best not when we predict when we'll be done, but when we *choose* when to be done and then ensure that we put the best features in by that date. The Natural Way lets you do that by selecting important features and building a releasable version every couple of weeks.

Whether we use estimated hours, story points, or just count stories, using velocity to project when we'll be "done" is nearly always a sign of dysfunction.

The premise of this book is that we want value, we want value soon, and we want highest value first. The best way to do this, as we've discussed, is always to be "done." If your organization has some fixed content in mind, toward which your team is working, you are likely "doing it wrong." You are likely not managing by value but by cost. This is a sucker's game.

Provide Real Opportunities to Upgrade Skills

(See also Chapter 14, *Creating Teams That Thrive*, on page 94.)

What really helps a team be more productive is higher skill. This means that your investment in training and education will pay off in productivity.

People work pretty hard. Is it sensible to imagine that they will then invest in their growth in the evening or on week-ends, out of their limited personal time? What can we do to make that more likely?

Most employees live on a fairly tight budget. Is it sensible to imagine that they'll use their own vacation time and money to take courses or attend valuable conferences? What can we do to make sure that time and money for learning are available and used?

Don't "whip the ponies." Help them improve.

CHAPTER 18

To Speed Up, Build with Skill

At first, when we set out to build a complete but tiny product in easy, small cycles, things will go badly. That's normal. Let's look at a few of the main things that can go wrong and what we can do about them. Think in terms of the style of these suggestions, not just the specifics.

Our team says: We can't get all these features done in two weeks.

Yes, this is a common problem. Often when starting out, a team can't deliver a fully integrated product increment in two weeks and will ask for more time. Instead of giving your team more time, I suggest giving them less. Ask your team to produce a fully integrated product increment in one week instead of two!

Chances are, they'll figure out how to do it. They'll see that they need to make just a few actual changes, and then focus their attention on getting those changes integrated, tested, and running.

Once in a while—and I see this more when talking about it than when doing it—the team will come to me and say, "We can't get anything done in a week." I generally ask them, "Well, can you get anything done in a day, then?" They'll reply that they can't, and I'll ask them why they plan to come in tomorrow if they aren't going to do anything. Ha, ha, very funny. Except I'm serious.

This generally gets the conversation aimed at why it's difficult to produce an increment. And once we're dealing with why, it's easy to figure out things to do. The answers usually come down to build times, integration times, and test times.

If the problems still aren't clear, let's ask the team to rebuild the system and get it ready to deploy without making any changes at all. If we can't do that in a week, we'll sure know where the problem is, won't we?

One way or another our software-building process is slow and unreliable. Great. We're computer programmers and we can fix that.

As Product Champion or manager, you want this fixed more than the team does. You need to see a completed product increment, and you need to see it on a regular basis. So there's incredibly high value in getting that increment built. That's why asking for a single feature, or a tiny feature, or even no feature at all is a good business decision. You're not asking them to focus on some technical thing: never do that. You're asking them to show you the software.

Our team says: We can't get anything ready for release until after "they" test it.

As your team's Product Champion or manager, you know that's just not acceptable. When defects come back from QA, they interfere with our business planning, because we have to do things over again and cannot focus our attention on our business purpose.

So the solution is very simple, and very difficult: When the team ships software to QA, we must already be certain that it will not be coming back with defects in it.

We do that by testing it ourselves. The technical practices of acceptance test-driven development (ATDD) and test-driven development (TDD) enable us to do this quite nicely. We can be increasingly confident that when we pass something on, it will work as desired. Our teams must be experts in ATDD and TDD.

Sometimes the external dependency is not on testing but on some other "resource," perhaps a DBA department or a user interface design department. The fix for this is to make your team cross-functional. That is, import these skills to your team. And the best way to do that is to assign people from those departments as real team members on our important projects.

But the team says: It still takes time to get really done.

That's OK. We want to take all the time needed to get done "the first time." Learning to build a solid product increment will take time, especially if our team is struggling with a load of code written in old-fashioned ways. That's not unsolvable. The Agile method Scrum has a notion that will help us here: the evolving "Definition of Done."

We need our team to produce a product increment in every "Sprint." That increment must meet the current Definition of Done. And the Definition of Done must become more stringent over time.

So in early cycles, we might not even require that the increment be integrated. We look at each feature one at a time, running on some developer's machine. This should make a business-side person Very Nervous: how do we know that these things will work together? So we improve our Definition of Done to say that all the features must work on a single development machine, in a single build. The team will have to take on fewer features for a bit while they get this to happen, but since we want them to show us the software, it's a good business decision.

Next, we may find that it's integrated, but it doesn't work very well. It needs more testing. So we add some testing criteria to our Definition of Done.

This will lead us to discover that we need to know at the beginning of the cycle how the software will be tested at the end. This leads us to get better at getting examples from the Product Champion, and to get better at building a common understanding of what we need.

And so it goes. With a single relentless focus on "show us the software," we improve the team's process so that when they take on some amount of work, they'll actually get it done.

Now we all say: It seems so SLOW!

It should feel slow at first. Later on, it will feel smooth and efficient, never rushed. We absolutely need a releasable, done, product increment every couple of weeks. To accomplish this, our work must be fully designed, fully tested, complete in every way. This means the team must take on less work in each cycle than we're used to. It will feel slow. The difference is, when we're done, we're really done.

Since we're getting closer to really done, the apparent slowness is an illusion. We're be eliminating most of that long, painful test-and-fix finish that wears on long after we were supposed to be done. Did you forget that little detail, all that time you spend after your application was supposed to launch, or after it does launch?

Second, since we're working incrementally, high value first, there's every chance to deliver useful value before the deadline. But we can only do that if the software actually works.

In early days, yes, it will feel slow. But even in early days, it may not really be slower: defects are being reduced, and cleaner code will keep the work flowing. Let it be. As your team gets good at really being done, they'll be able to take on more and more features, and things will improve more and more.

Summary

The most valuable thing you can do to speed up development is to build skill in the development team. That investment will pay off rapidly in less time lost to fixing defects, and in smoother development. Don't confuse thrashing with effective performance. The fastest teams move smoothly and gracefully.

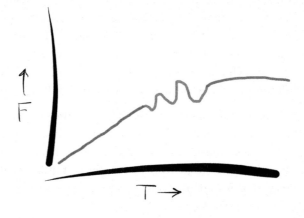

CHAPTER 19

Refactoring

Reminder: We need steady progress. To keep progress steady, we need a clear, clean design all the time. To accomplish this, we must refactor.

The Natural Way asks us to show steady progress in terms of visible, working software. Seeing real software come into being at a steady pace gives us a sense of where we are. This helps us decide what to do next and what to defer until later.

Often, though, our pace is not steady. Even though our work items seem all about equally difficult, our pace may become erratic. Shortly after this happens, our pace almost inevitably slows down.

This is demoralizing. Even worse, it makes planning difficult. Worse still, we'll usually see an increase in defects as this happens. And worst of all, our ability to get the best possible product by our deadline is at risk.

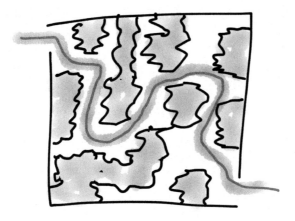

Twisty little passages

The time needed to build a feature comes from two main components: its inherent difficulty, and the accidental difficulty of putting it into whatever code already exists. Teams are good at estimating the inherent difficulty. What makes us erratic, what makes us slow down, is the accidental difficulty. We call this difficulty "bad code."

If we allow code quality to decline, some features go in easily, sailing right through. Others that seem similar get entangled in twisty little passages of bad code. Similar work starts taking radically different amounts of time.

To keep progress steady, we have to avoid building twisty little passages, and when we do build them, we need to straighten them out.

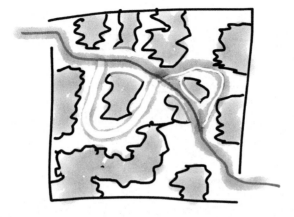

Refactoring straightens the passages.

The word *refactoring* refers to a simple, regular process of keeping the code clean. We try not to create the twisty little passages that slow us down. When twists do crop up, we straighten them out.

It's easy to cause our teams to skimp on refactoring: all we have to do is put them under pressure to get a few more features done than they realistically can. When we do that, they turn secret programmer dials called Not Enough Testing and Coding Shortcuts, and the result is that there are more defects, erratic progress, and, ultimately, a slowdown.

Bad work is hard to see. We can't see it from the outside: it's under the surface. But as businesspeople we need the work to be good. We should expect and demand that the team keeps the code clean. And if we notice erratic progress or a slowdown, it's probably time to bear down on cleaning things up again. That means it's time to lighten up on the pressure.

What to do when the passages have gotten all twisty

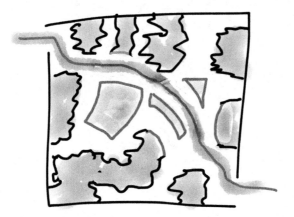

It's usually not a good idea to start over on some huge part of the product. It might be, but I'd bet it isn't.

It's usually not a good idea to stop doing features entirely, to "clean up" the code. It might be, but I'd bet it isn't.

What seems to work best is to follow the *Campground Rule: Leave the campground a little better than you found it.* Every time we do a feature, we start by cleaning up the area where we are going to do the work. We don't have to make it perfect, just sufficiently better to help our feature ease in. And once our feature works, we clean up the code as we always should—plus a bit more.

This process does just what we need: areas where we do little work aren't slowing us down, and they are left mostly alone. Areas where we do lots of work get more attention; they clean up quickly.

It's always tempting to developers to start over and rewrite. It's almost never the best plan. Instead, get good at refactoring, and apply the *Campground Rule.*

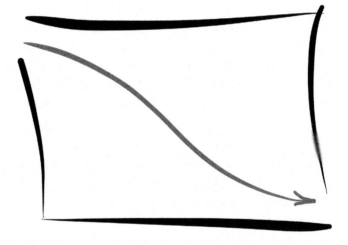

CHAPTER 20

Agile Methods

I am, by good fortune, one of the authors of the Agile Manifesto.[1] The story I tell here is in accord with the Manifesto, to the best of my ability. The "Natural Way" is a distillation of what I've learned in a half-century of software development and almost twenty years of doing "Agile." I am not trying to create another Agile method here. In *Nature*, I'm describing how I think software should be built, based on everything I've learned, before, during, and after "Agile."

If you want to know more about Agile software development, there are many Agile methods or frameworks out there. The most popular is surely Scrum, by Jeff Sutherland and Ken Schwaber. Scrum, by design, is not focused solely on software. As such, Scrum does not explicitly include technical practices such as acceptance test-driven development, test-driven development, refactoring, and so on. I'm here to tell you that to prosper, you'll need to add those practices to your Scrum projects.

XP, or Extreme Programming, created by Kent Beck, is a framework that does explicitly include those technical practices. Otherwise, XP is much like Scrum. XP does not include the Scrum-specific "ScrumMaster" role, but it often recommends a coach, which is a similar notion. To me, Scrum plus technical practices amounts to XP. Some people would disagree with me on that.

Alistair Cockburn's Crystal Clear is an Agile framework that is even simpler than Scrum. There are also complex large-

---

1.   http://agilemanifesto.org

scale Agile-like frameworks, such as Dynamic Systems Development Method (DSDM), Larman/Vodde's Large Scale Scrum (LeSS), Scott Ambler's Disciplined Agile Development (DAD), or Dean Leffingwell's Scaled Agile Framework (SAFe). And many more. Read about them if you're interested.

Again, *The Nature of Software Development* does not describe Yet Another Agile Framework. Instead, I invite you to think about what needs to go on in any software project, especially any would-be "Agile" software project, so that you can be successful working in whatever framework you choose.

I do have some advice about frameworks, however:

- Try to have too little framework, not too much. Don't even have "enough." As the Agile Manifesto says, we prefer "individuals and interactions over processes and tools." A framework for your project wants to fit loosely, more like a sweat suit than like spandex. Everyone on the project needs room to "slosh around freely," to interact in ways that are not contemplated by any framework and that cannot be dictated by rules.

- Keep it light. Naturally, if you have a large project, with many teams, you'll need more process than if you have just six people in a team room somewhere. But even so, keep it light. Use retrospectives to decide what kinds of additions to make. Add process elements as experiments. Be clear what you expect to get from the change, and check to see if you get it. If you don't, or you get some undesirable additional effect, make a different change next time.

- Control the framework; don't let the framework control you. Modify your framework to make your projects more effective. However, don't change the framework just because it asks you to do difficult things. The ideas in this book, and the ideas in your framework, are there to challenge you to improve. Adjust things to your abilities—but stretch yourself a bit.

- Keep process changes close to the team. There's no advantage to imposing practices worldwide. You are managing your project by observing the actual running software, coming out feature by feature, correctly executing verification tests that the business defines. You are determining what goes on inside your teams by observing their results, and the pace of producing results. You don't need to demand specific process elements, and doing so will backfire.

- Make learning a priority. As we see in this book, skills are required at all levels of the project, from the highest business elements, through the management, right down to the technical people. The technical people, in particular, work with the software every day, and they need to have specific skills to do it well. Expect to invest in training and support for your project. It will pay off in faster delivery of better software.

- Most of all, think. The work of building a valuable product is complex, and it is best accomplished, not by trying to anticipate and control everything, but by observing what happens and responding to events. It's a bit like a team sport: there may be plans, there may even be planned plays. But what happens in the game is always different, and success lies in the ability of the team members to interact in the moment. Paradoxically, our ability to seize the moment comes from the thinking we do before the action starts. Think.

You don't need to "scale" Agile. You just need to do it.

CHAPTER 21

Scaling Agile

There's a lot of interest in "scaling" Agile these days, and it has become big business. Large companies have heard the clarion call of the Agile Buzzword, and just as they did with past good ideas like Six Sigma and TQM, now they want to go Agile. It has become the thing to do. But they're large companies. So, naturally, they think they need to scale.

It turns out that in most cases, they're wrong. They don't need to scale. They need to do plain old simple Agile software development.

CALING

Scaling Agile is good business for scaling vendors. It's not necessarily good advice for you.

Scaling Agile has become a good business to be in, because people think they need it. There has always been a decent market for scaling Agile, so there have always been some contending approaches to doing it. Now, with the market for Big Agile growing, there are even more.

I'll leave it to you to look those up and choose among them if you must. What I'd like to do here is to suggest that—with one possible exception—these approaches are misguided.

That's not to say that large-scale Agile won't be successful; very likely it will be. It will be successful in the sense that large companies will buy scaling products and ideas, and consultants and training companies will enrich themselves selling what these large companies want.

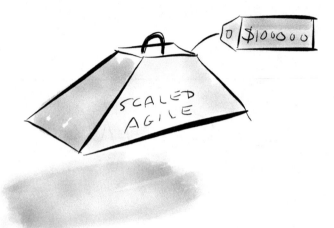

As the Rolling Stones remind us, you can't always get what you want.

Unfortunately, contrary to the song, a big company can always get what it wants—in this case lots of expensive training in some heavy approach that touts itself as Scaled Agile. And they'll get some benefit, certainly. Any attention to improvement is usually better than no attention at all. And to the extent that these various approaches include some real Agile ideas, organizations will get some of that as well.

I'm here to talk about what the song offers: I'm here to talk about what you need. What does a large company really need to know about applying Agile ideas throughout?

Agile is simple—it just isn't easy.

Agile is quite simple. The most popular Agile approach, Scrum, has just three roles, a handful of activities, and one major artifact: running tested software.

That doesn't mean Agile is easy. It's still hard to decide what product would be desirable, and it's still hard to write software that does what is asked for. It is, however, quite simple. Simplicity is the essence of what makes up Agility. So if Agile is simple, what about so-called scaled Agile?

Scaled Agile must be simple—or it isn't Agile.

Chet Hendrickson points out that since Agile is simple, a scaled version of Agile should also be that simple, or even simpler. Otherwise, it will no longer be Agile. We should look with great suspicion at a so-called "Scaled Agile" approach that is complex.

Along the same lines, Arlo Belshee suggests that if all your development teams have become fluent in Agile software development, scaling is not a problem. If all your teams can slice stories small, select a number that they can accomplish in a Sprint (or otherwise within time estimates), and deliver integrated software that is free of defects, then "scaling" should be easy. Diana Larsen and Jim Shore, originators of the notion of fluency in this context, make similar points.

Let's explore this. Agile is simple (but not easy). If your individual teams could really execute software development in the Agile style, might "Scaling Agile" be easy?

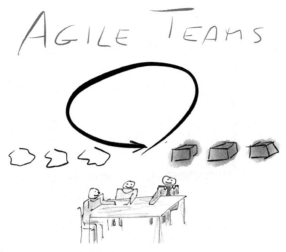

If your teams are truly Agile…

Agile teams work daily with their business-side associates (Agile Manifesto Principle 4). They deliver working software frequently, every couple of weeks (Principle 3). They measure themselves with working software (Principle 7), work in a sustainable fashion (Principle 8), and pay constant attention to technical excellence and good design (Principle 9). And so on.

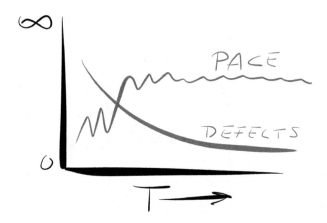

...I mean truly Agile...

Fluent Agile teams, after just a little jostling when they start up, produce a consistent flow of features, and they drive defects down to levels far below what the same team accomplished before they became fluent in Agile.

Fluent Agile teams are visibly Agile, visibly fluent. They get things truly done, at a consistent and predictable pace. If your teams are up to that...

...you might already be done.

So there you are. All your teams are capable of producing working software, every two weeks, working daily with the business-side people who describe what the team needs to build.

You might be done scaling Agile, if everything your organization builds can be built by a single Agile team.

Really. Think about this for a moment. If everything you do could be built by a single small team, scaling Agile comes down to having each team learn to build in the Agile fashion, then hooking them up with a business-side person to guide what they build.

Done. Agile Scaled. No extra work beyond the basics. The basics are hard enough of course. We've explored that elsewhere in the book. But there's no big corporate rollout/transition/Enterprise Agile that you need to do.

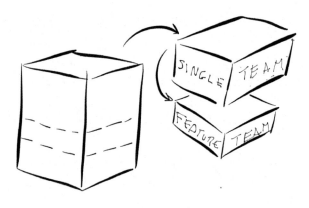

What if you want more than one team can do?

A single Agile team that can really do this stuff produces multiple features every couple of weeks. It's not easy to keep even one team working at capacity: you have to have a lot of product ideas to do it. But maybe you have a huge product, like a word processor or some graphics program for editing photographs. You feel there is enough work there to keep multiple teams busy.

Well, first of all, prove it. Get a single team working on your product up to Agile quality. Then look at the rate at which they deliver features. See if you really need more features than that. Odds are, you won't: your customers probably can't absorb new capability faster than a single team can deliver. But maybe there is enough work to keep more than one team busy.

Aha! Now we'll have to scale Agile...won't we?

Feature teams

Well, maybe not. Way back in the last century, the idea of the feature team was devised. A feature team is a small team whose job it is to deliver features into a product. To get more features, you add more feature teams, all delivering software into a single product. Want more features per unit time? Add another feature team, get more features.

There's not much involved in scaling this way, is there? If every team knows how to do what a real Agile team knows how to do, you can add feature teams, and any product made of features can go as fast as you want.

Aren't we skipping something? How do those teams coordinate? Now we've got multiple teams doing features. How can they avoid stepping on each other's toes?

Agile teams coordinate using tests.

Remember that Agile teams do a large number of small features every two weeks. A single team can easily do fifteen or twenty such features in a two-week iteration. How do they manage not to get in each other's way?

It turns out to be simple. Fluent Agile teams build a growing container of automated checks, using acceptance test-driven development and test-driven development. These checks help teams know when they have completed a feature. However, they also serve as a growing collection of regression checks that ensure all the features built keep on working.

If we're using multiple feature teams, it works the same way. Each team, every time it builds a new small feature, adds that feature, with its automated checks, into the common codebase. All the teams do this daily, just as a single team would. They keep all the checks running, all the time. If from time to time a team tries to check something in and tests fail, they fix the problem before checking in so that the current codebase always runs all the checks.

Might there be a conflict between things done across teams? Possibly, and if that happens, the teams coordinate to see what happened. But the general practice is quite simple: if the checks were running before you put your change in, and they're not running after you put your change in, your change broke something. You find that something, and fix it, so that all the checks run—yours plus all the historical ones.

Agile teams do this as a matter of course. They learn to do smaller and smaller releases. When they use small releases, the chance that they break something is very small. When (rarely) they do break something, it's easy to find the issue, because only a small amount of code has been added or changed.

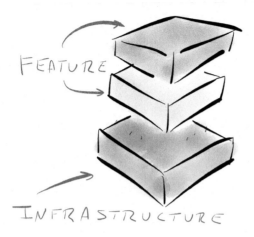

FEATURE

INFRASTRUCTURE

OK, feature teams, but what about infrastructure?

If your product is really big enough to use multiple feature teams, they'll be relying on some common infrastructure. What about changes to that?

Same way. Agile teams change their infrastructure as needed. They do so freely, every couple of weeks, by supporting their changes with automated checks. Feature teams can do the same thing, with each team making the changes it needs, adding checks to the pool, and checking in code frequently.

Will you need a specialized infrastructure team? Quite often, if you're fluent in Agile, you won't. Specialist teams very often dissolve in an Agile situation. But if you do choose to have such a team, and they're Agile, they can smoothly produce infrastructure changes, supported by automated checks, in support of multiple feature teams. I recommend letting your feature teams handle infrastructure changes, coordinating among themselves as needed. But if you do choose to have a specialized team for infrastructure, despite that advice, there's still no need for special scaling.

Remember, it's unlikely that you'll need feature teams at all if your individual teams can do Agile. But if you do, you won't need any special infrastructure to have feature teams—you just need multiple empowered teams who can, and will, coordinate among themselves as needed.

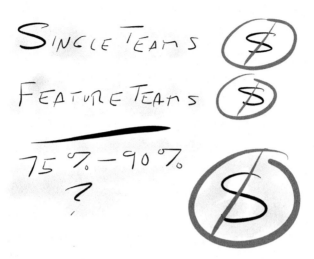

So far, so good

A company whose work can be done by a single team does not need anything special to scale Agile. A company with a need for more features than a single team can handle can build feature teams, and they won't need anything else to scale their Agile process.

In most organizations I've seen, the majority of the work is done by single teams already. In a few, I have seen a product that is integrated enough, and large enough, where feature teams might be needed. What else is there?

Giant efforts

Some companies undertake truly large efforts, with hundreds of developers, perhaps even thousands, all working on one thing. If you're not in a company like that, maybe all you need is to get your individual teams able to operate in an Agile fashion. You could stop reading now, or jump to the conclusion. But you're probably wondering what to do about giant efforts.

First, grow the giant incrementally.

If you're starting a giant effort, even one built on existing architecture, the standard Agile approach works. Start with a single team. Build it larger and larger. Build and extend infrastructure as you go. Add feature teams as you need them.

Finally, divide the giant, mostly along feature teams.

Even in giant efforts, it turns out that almost everything being done is being done by single teams. We already know how to do those: standard Agile. Just do that.

Even in giant efforts, a few efforts can be improved by adding more working teams. Do that, and operate them like feature teams. Standard Agile. Just do that.

What's left? Is there really something, somewhere, that needs more than one team, and that can't be divided up into smaller efforts that can be done in Agile fashion?

In most cases, I doubt it. I don't think there are giant efforts that are truly irreducible. If there are, no one knows how to do them, Agile or not. The very essence of putting lots of people on an effort is to divide up the work. If we do not know how to divide up the work, adding people will not help.

If we do know how to divide up the work, then, almost always, the bulk of the work can be done using standard Agile. Is there enough left to require a complex approach to scaling? Perhaps. Wait and see; that's my advice.

Bottom line

If your individual teams cannot work in an Agile fashion, then clearly you're not ready to "transition" your company or to "scale" Agile. You don't want to transition to something you can't do, and you don't want to scale something that doesn't work.

First, start creating teams that are very capable of doing Agile.

Then, give them the most important, most valuable work to do that your organization can come up with. And stand back.

Keep creating Agile teams, organized by features where possible. You may find that you have little need to scale Agile. More likely, you just have to do it.

CHAPTER 22

Conclusion

If you've made it all the way here, congratulations! Let me sum up what I believe we've just been through, to help you settle in your mind just what has happened here.

Imagine that you're climbing a mountain called Software Development. Maybe you're a beginner, down near the bottom, walking up steep trails, once in a while clambering over rocks. Maybe you're pretty advanced, with a whole kit of climbing equipment and knowledge. Maybe you even help others with their own climbing journey. Maybe you're one of those amazing free climbers who can lift yourself from a single hand jam and kick your foot over your head to find the next tiny crevice in what looks like a wall of glass.

Whatever your level, if you're like me, you spend a lot of time looking at the mountain face right in front of your nose. You spend a lot of time using your mind to figure out your next move upward and which muscles you'll use to make the move.

This book is some words and pictures from someone on the same mountain, who has found a reasonably flat and pleasant place to sit and look around for a while. He looks outward and sees the amazing vista that's almost always out of sight behind our back as we climb. He looks down the mountain and sees its shape and sees the climbers moving upward, some not as well as he did, some much better. He sees the paths on the mountain and can tell which ones are easy, which ones are hard, which ones are safe, and which ones are dangerous.

Then he looks up, and through the clouds and haze, he realizes that there's more climbing to do, lots more, as we work our way upward. He sees what look like likely paths and other interesting spots to stop and look around.

He takes some pictures of what he sees and writes a few words about his thoughts and discoveries. He sketches a few paths and tells you a bit about how he recognizes a good path, and what he does when a path turns out not so good. He offers all this to you, to enrich your own journey up the mountain, to remind you of the many beautiful views that make the hard climb worthwhile. He reminds you that sometimes the reward is just in the climbing itself, doing it more and more well.

He says, "Here's what it all looks like to me. What does it look like to you?"

Thanks for reading!

Bibliography

[Pin09]   Daniel H. Pink. *Drive: The Surprising Truth About What Motivates Us*. Riverhead Books, New York, NY, USA, 2009.

[Pir00]   Robert M. Pirsig. *Zen and the Art of Motorcycle Maintenance: An Inquiry into Values*. Perennial Classics, New York, NY, USA, Reprint Edition, 2000.

Index

A

acceptance test-driven development, 66, 73, 117, 126, 140

activity-based planning, 20–22

adjusting direction, xv, 11, 45, 108

Agile, *see also* scaling; Scrum
  Agile Manifesto, 126–127
  defining value, 80–81
  methods, viii, 126–128
  resources, 126

Ambler, Scott, 126

architecture, *see* foundations; infrastructure

automated tests, 66–67, 73, 140

autonomy, 94, 96

B

Beck, Kent, 37, 126

Belshee, Arlo, 134

blame, 117–118

budget
  management decisions, 101, 106
  planning feature by feature, 34

bugs, *see* defects

building
  eliminating test-and-fix interval, 48
  by features, 5, 42–49, 77

  features and foundations in parallel, 51–59
  identifying progress, 47
  refining design while, 49
  refining features, 57
  small cycles, 44
  value pyramid, 5, 77

business-level tests, 65–66, 68

business-side personnel, *see also* Product Champion
  building features and foundations in parallel, 59
  Natural Way benefits, xv
  planning with stories, 36
  purpose, 95
  refining product vision, 45

C

Campground Rule, 124

coaches, 126

Cockburn, Alistair, 126

code, refactoring, 122–124

Communities of Practice, 29–30

conferences, 115

consensus, 87

continuous planning, 36, 41

continuous testing, 60–68, 73, 77

controlling
  frameworks, 127
  management component, 101, 109

coordinating, multiple teams, 139–147

costs
  design deterioration, 73
  monolithic projects, 22
  planning feature by feature, 34
  value by feature, 13

Crystal Clear, 126

cycles
  building in small, 44
  improvement and difficulty, 91
  perception of slowness, 116–119

D

DAD (Disciplined Agile Development), 126

deadlines
  planning by, 19
  stopping before, 34, 105

defects
  building by features, 48
  planning and, 21
  pressure, 39, 112–115, 123
  quality and value pyramid, 5, 77
  speed, 39, 63–64, 68
  stretch goals, 39

delays
    defects, 63–64, 112
    evaluating, 113–114
delegating, 101, 107, 110
delivery
    building by features,
        5
    building features and
        foundations in par-
        allel, 58
    value of early deliv-
        ery, xiii, 8–11, 15,
        77
DeMarco, Tom, 63
design, *see also* founda-
    tions; infrastructure
    deterioration, 70, 73
    quality, 5, 77
    refactoring, 72–73,
        77, 120–124
    refining while build-
        ing by features, 49
    simplicity, 69
    testing, 60–68, 73, 77
deterioration, design, 70,
    73
developers, *see* teams
directing, management
    component, 101, 108
direction, changing, xv,
    11, 45, 108
Disciplined Agile Develop-
    ment (DAD), 126
done, definition of
    building feature by
        feature, 46–47
    eliminating test-and-
        fix interval, 48, 119
    identifying progress,
        47
    mastery and, 97
    pressure for speed,
        114, 118
Drive, 94
Drucker, Peter, 101
Dynamic Systems Develop-
    ment Method (DSDM),
    126

E

ease *vs.* simplicity, xvi, 88–
    91, 93, 133–137
end users, xv

estimating, *see also* forecast-
    ing
    disadvantages, 34–
        35, 38
    pressure for speed,
        113–114
    work pieces, 37
    working without, 40
experts and specialists
    feature teams, 29–30
    infrastructure teams
        for large projects,
        142
    team productivity,
        113
external dependencies, 117
Extreme Programming,
    126

F

feature teams, defined,
    139, *see also* teams
features, *see also* testing
    asking for, 117
    building by, 5, 42–49,
        77
    building foundations
        first, 54
    building in parallel
        with foundations,
        51–59
    forecasting with
        "Five-Card
        Method", 99
    guiding by, 19–24
    minimal marketable
        features (MMFs),
        12
    organizing by, 5, 26–
        31, 77
    planning by, 5, 19–
        24, 32–41, 77
    prioritizing, 24, 46,
        57, 99, 103–104
    refining multiple iter-
        ations, 57
    separating delivery,
        9–10
    slicing, 5, 40, 99
    small cycles, 44
    splitting, 36
    value and, 7, 12–16,
        77
"Five-Card Method", 99
fluency and scaling Agile,
    134–137
forecasting, 99, *see also* esti-
    mating

foundations, *see also* de-
    sign; infrastructure
    building first, 54
    building in parallel
        with features, 51–
        59
    importance of, 52
Fowler, Martin, 37
frameworks, 126–128

G

game, lava, xii–xiv
giant projects, 144–147
goals, stretch, 39
guiding
    feature by feature,
        19–24
    value pyramid, 5, 77

H

Hendrickson, Chet, 134
hiring policy, 107

I

information
    changing direction, 11
    Natural Way benefits,
        xv
    planning feature by
        feature, 24
    stopping delivery, 11
infrastructure, *see also* de-
    sign; foundations
    building in parallel
        with features, 51–
        59
    multiple teams for
        large projects, 142
"Inspect and Adapt"
    mantra, 97
iterations
    building in small cy-
        cles, 44
    continuous testing,
        66–68
    mastery, 97
    perception of slow-
        ness, 116–119
    planning workload,
        37
    prioritizing features,
        46
    refining features, 57

L

Large Scale Scrum (LeSS), 126

Larman, Craig, 126

Larsen, Diana, 134

lava game, xii–xiv

learning, 128, 147, *see also* training

Leffingwell, Dean, 126

LeSS (Large Scale Scrum), 126

limiting products and programs, 102

long-term planning, 102, 108

M

management
  budget decisions, 101, 106
  control component, 101, 109
  defining value, 83
  direction component, 101, 108
  Natural Way benefits, xv
  need for, 100
  organizational decisions, 101, 106
  planning component, 101–105
  pressure and defects, 112–115
  staffing decisions, 101, 106
  team purpose, autonomy, and mastery, 94–97

mastery, 94, 97

measuring, value, 84–87

mid-term planning, 103

minimal marketable features (MMFs), 12

minimum viable product, 56

monolithic projects, 20–22

multiple teams, disadvantages, 26, 28

N

Natural Way
  Agile methods, 126

summary of benefits, xv–xvi
  wandering path, xiii, 93

O

observing, teams, 5

organizing
  by features, 5, 26–31, 77
  management component, 101, 106
  self-organizing teams, 96–97, 101, 106
  value pyramid, 5, 77

P

Pink, Daniel, 94

Pirsig, Robert, 80

planning
  activity-based, 20–22
  continuous, 36, 41
  by features, 5, 19–24, 32–41, 77
  "Five-Card Method", 99
  level of detail, 34
  long-term, 102, 108
  as management component, 101–105
  mid-term, 103
  multiple releases, 22
  need for, 33
  risk, 23, 38
  short-term, 104
  starting, 35
  stretch goals, 39
  team workload, 37
  value pyramid, 5, 77
  without estimates, 40

predictability, planning feature by feature, 23

pressure
  defects, 39, 112–115, 123
  definition of done, 114, 118
  stretch goals, 39

prioritizing
  features, 24, 46, 57, 99, 103–104
  learning, 128
  value, xiv, 86, 88, 93, 105

Product Champion
  control component, 109
  defining purpose, 95

defining value, 83, 85
  management support of, 108
  organizing teams by features, 27
  planning feature by feature, 37
  product vision, 100
  selecting features, 59
  selecting team members, 106

productivity
  experts and specialists, 113
  increasing, 113–115
  team purpose, autonomy, and mastery, 94–97

professional development, *see* training

programmer tests, 65, 67

progress, identifying, 47

purpose, 94–95

pyramid of value, 5, 77

Q

quality
  continuous testing, 60–68, 73, 77
  planning and, 21
  pressure for speed, 113
  refactoring, 122–124
  value pyramid, 5, 77

questions
  budget, 34
  building by features, 43–47, 49
  building features and foundations in parallel, 52, 59
  delivery, 8–11
  estimating, 35, 38
  features, 12–16, 99
  identifying progress, 47
  planning, 19–24, 33–36, 38–39, 99
  pressure, 39
  product vision, 45
  quality, 21
  refining design, 49
  small cycles, 44
  splitting features, 36
  team skills, 59
  value, 7

R

refactoring, 72–73, 77, 120–124, 126

refining
design while building by features, 49
features in multiple iterations, 57
product vision, 45

regression checks, 140

releases, multiple
planning for, 22
separating features, 10

responsibility
autonomy and, 96
delegating management, 110

return on investment, xv

risk
estimations, 38
planning feature by feature, 23, 38

S

Scaled Agile Framework (SAFe), 126

scaling
giant projects, 144–147
market for, 131
misunderstanding need for, 130–132
multiple teams, 138–147
organizing teams by features, 31
simplicity vs. ease, 133–137

Schwaber, Ken, 126

scope, planning and estimating, 38

Scrum
Definition of Done, 118
"Inspect and Adapt" mantra, 97
practices, 126
simplicity, 133

ScrumMaster, 126

shepherding, 30

Shore, Jim, 134

short-term planning, 104

simplicity
building features and foundations in parallel, 56
design, 69
vs. ease, xvi, 88–91, 93, 133–137
scaled Agile, 133–137

size
budget and, 106
design, 49
features, 40, 99
forecasting, 99
planning, 102–103

skills
building features and foundations in parallel, 59
building speed with, 116–119
mastery, 94, 97
team productivity, 113–114

slicing
features, 40, 99
Scaling Agile, 134
value pyramid, 5

slowness, perception of, 116–119

specialists, see experts and specialists

speed
building features and foundations in parallel, 53–58
building with skills, 116–119
continuous testing, 68
defects, 39, 63–64, 68, 112–115
definition of done, 114, 118
design deterioration, 70, 73
refining design while building by features, 49

splitting features, 36

sprints
defined, 36
definition of done, 118
planning, 36

staff, see teams

staffing decisions, 101, 106–107

steering, 105

stopping
before deadline, 34, 105
value of, 11, 15

stories, planning, 36

stretch goals, 39

Sutherland, Jeff, 126

T

tasks, planning, 36

TDD (test-driven development), 67, 73, 117, 126, 140

teams
Communities of Practice, 30
experts and specialists, 29–30, 113, 142
fluency and scaling Agile, 134–137
guiding, 5
increasing productivity, 113
multiple teams and disadvantages, 26, 28
multiple teams and scaling Agile, 138–147
Natural Way benefits, xv
organizing by features, 26–31
process changes, 128
purpose, autonomy, and mastery, 94–97
self-organizing teams, 96–97, 101, 106
staffing decisions, 101, 106–107
workload planning, 37

test-driven development (TDD), 67, 73, 117, 126, 140

testing
acceptance test-driven development, 66, 73, 117, 126, 140
automated, 66–67, 73, 140
business-level tests, 65–66, 68
continuous, 60–68, 73, 77
coordinating multiple teams, 140–147

eliminating test-and-fix interval, 48, 119
monolithic projects, 20–21
programmer tests, 65, 67
Scrum, 126
speed and, 117
test-driven development (TDD), 67, 73, 117, 126, 140
thinking, *see also* questions; value
drawing pictures, ix
as mountain, 148–149
need for, xvi, 128
time
defects, 63, 68
eliminating test-and-fix interval, 48, 119
organizing by skill, 28

planning feature by feature, 34
value by feature, 13
training
expertise and feature teams, 29
increasing productivity, 114
prioritizing, 128
scaling training programs, 132

V
vacations, 115
value
defining, 7, 80–83, 85
delivering early, xiii, 8–11, 15, 77
features, 7, 12–16, 77
focus on, xiv, 86, 88, 93, 105
measuring, 84–87

overview, 5
prioritizing features, 46, 99
pyramid, 5, 77
of stopping, 11, 15
summary, 77
vision, refining, 45
Vodde, Bas, 126

W
whipping the ponies, 112–115

X
XP, 126

Y
"Yesterday's Weather", 37

Z
Zen and the Art of Motorcycle Maintenance, 80

Explore Testing and Cucumber

Explore the uncharted waters of exploratory testing and beef up your automated testing with more Cucumber—now for Java, too.

Explore It!

Uncover surprises, risks, and potentially serious bugs with exploratory testing. Rather than designing all tests in advance, explorers design and execute small, rapid experiments, using what they learned from the last little experiment to inform the next. Learn essential skills of a master explorer, including how to analyze software to discover key points of vulnerability, how to design experiments on the fly, how to hone your observation skills, and how to focus your efforts.

Explisabeth Hendrickson
Edited by Jacquelyn Carter

Elisabeth Hendrickson
(160 pages) ISBN: 9781937785024. $29
https://pragprog.com/book/ehxta

The Cucumber for Java Book

Teams working on the JVM can now say goodbye forever to misunderstood requirements, tedious manual acceptance tests, and out-of-date documentation. Cucumber—the popular, open-source tool that helps teams communicate more effectively with their customers—now has a Java version, and our bestselling *Cucumber Book* has been updated to match. *The Cucumber for Java Book* has the same great advice about how to deliver rock-solid applications collaboratively, but with all code completely rewritten in Java. New chapters cover features unique to the Java version of Cucumber, and reflect insights from the Cucumber team since the original book was published.

Seb Rose, Matt Wynne & Aslak Hellesoy
(250 pages) ISBN: 9781941222294. $36
https://pragprog.com/book/srjcuc

Be Agile

Don't just "do" agile; you want to *be* agile. We'll show you how to make software better.

Your Code As a Crime Scene

Jack the Ripper and legacy codebases have more in common than you'd think. Inspired by forensic psychology methods, this book teaches you strategies to predict the future of your codebase, assess refactoring direction, and understand how your team influences the design. With its unique blend of forensic psychology and code analysis, this book arms you with the strategies you need, no matter what programming language you use.

Adam Tornhill
(190 pages) ISBN: 9781680500387. $36
https://pragprog.com/book/atcrime

The Agile Samurai

Here are three simple truths about software development:

1. You can't gather all the requirements up front.
2. The requirements you do gather will change.
3. There is always more to do than time and money will allow.

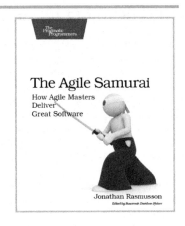

Those are the facts of life. But you can deal with those facts (and more) by becoming a fierce software-delivery professional, capable of dispatching the most dire of software projects and the toughest delivery schedules with ease and grace.

This title is also available as an audio book.

Jonathan Rasmusson
(280 pages) ISBN: 9781934356586. $34.95
https://pragprog.com/book/jtrap

Past and Present

To see where we're going, remember how we got here, and learn how to take a healthier approach to programming.

Fire in the Valley

In the 1970s, while their contemporaries were protesting the computer as a tool of dehumanization and oppression, a motley collection of college dropouts, hippies, and electronics fanatics were engaged in something much more subversive. Obsessed with the idea of getting computer power into their own hands, they launched from their garages a hobbyist movement that grew into an industry, and ultimately a social and technological revolution. What they did was invent the personal computer: not just a new device, but a watershed in the relationship between man and machine. This is their story.

Michael Swaine and Paul Freiberger
(424 pages) ISBN: 9781937785765. $34
https://pragprog.com/book/fsfire

The Healthy Programmer

To keep doing what you love, you need to maintain your own systems, not just the ones you write code for. Regular exercise and proper nutrition help you learn, remember, concentrate, and be creative—skills critical to doing your job well. Learn how to change your work habits, master exercises that make working at a computer more comfortable, and develop a plan to keep fit, healthy, and sharp for years to come.

This book is intended only as an informative guide for those wishing to know more about health issues. In no way is this book intended to replace, countermand, or conflict with the advice given to you by your own healthcare provider including Physician, Nurse Practitioner, Physician Assistant, Registered Dietician, and other licensed professionals.

Joe Kutner
(254 pages) ISBN: 9781937785314. $36
https://pragprog.com/book/jkthp

Redesign Your Career

Ready to kick your career up to the next level? Time to rewire your brain and then reinvigorate your job itself.

Pragmatic Thinking and Learning

Software development happens in your head. Not in an editor, IDE, or design tool. You're well educated on how to work with software and hardware, but what about *wetware*—our own brains? Learning new skills and new technology is critical to your career, and it's all in your head.

In this book by Andy Hunt, you'll learn how our brains are wired, and how to take advantage of your brain's architecture. You'll learn new tricks and tips to learn more, faster, and retain more of what you learn.

You need a pragmatic approach to thinking and learning. You need to *Refactor Your Wetware*.

Printed in full color.

Andy Hunt
(252 pages) ISBN: 9781934356050. $34.95
https://pragprog.com/book/ahptl

The Passionate Programmer (2nd edition)

This book is about creating a remarkable career in software development. In most cases, remarkable careers don't come by chance. They require thought, intention, action, and a willingness to change course when you've made mistakes. Most of us have been stumbling around letting our careers take us where they may. It's time to take control. This revised and updated second edition lays out a strategy for planning and creating a radically successful life in software development.

Chad Fowler
(232 pages) ISBN: 9781934356340. $23.95
https://pragprog.com/book/cfcar2

Make it Work

Do retrospectives the right way, and see how to get new ideas accepted.

Agile Retrospectives

See how to mine the experience of your software development team continually throughout the life of the project. The tools and recipes in this book will help you uncover and solve hidden (and not-so-hidden) problems with your technology, your methodology, and those difficult "people issues" on your team.

Esther Derby and Diana Larsen, Foreword by Ken Schwaber
(200 pages) ISBN: 9780977616640. $29.95
https://pragprog.com/book/dlret

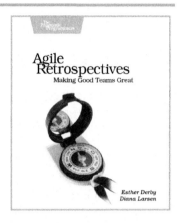

Driving Technical Change

If you work with people, you need this book. Learn to read co-workers' and users' *patterns of resistance* and dismantle their objections. With these techniques and strategies you can master the art of evangelizing and help your organization adopt your solutions.

Terrence Ryan
(146 pages) ISBN: 9781934356609. $32.95
https://pragprog.com/book/trevan

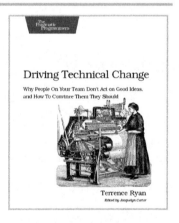

The Pragmatic Bookshelf

The Pragmatic Bookshelf features books written by developers for developers. The titles continue the well-known Pragmatic Programmer style and continue to garner awards and rave reviews. As development gets more and more difficult, the Pragmatic Programmers will be there with more titles and products to help you stay on top of your game.

Visit Us Online

This Book's Home Page
https://pragprog.com/book/rjnsd
Source code from this book, errata, and other resources. Come give us feedback, too!

Register for Updates
https://pragprog.com/updates
Be notified when updates and new books become available.

Join the Community
https://pragprog.com/community
Read our weblogs, join our online discussions, participate in our mailing list, interact with our wiki, and benefit from the experience of other Pragmatic Programmers.

New and Noteworthy
https://pragprog.com/news
Check out the latest pragmatic developments, new titles and other offerings.

Save on the eBook

Save on the eBook versions of this title. Owning the paper version of this book entitles you to purchase the electronic versions at a terrific discount.

PDFs are great for carrying around on your laptop—they are hyperlinked, have color, and are fully searchable. Most titles are also available for the iPhone and iPod touch, Amazon Kindle, and other popular e-book readers.

Buy now at *https://pragprog.com/coupon*

Contact Us

Online Orders:	*https://pragprog.com/catalog*
Customer Service:	*support@pragprog.com*
International Rights:	*translations@pragprog.com*
Academic Use:	*academic@pragprog.com*
Write for Us:	*http://write-for-us.pragprog.com*
Or Call:	+1 800-699-7764

CPSIA information can be obtained at www.ICGtesting.com
Printed in the USA
BVOW11s2044021115

425277BV00003B/8/P

9 781941 222379